New Ways in  ...hip

New Ways in Christian Worship

Robert W. Bailey

BROADMAN PRESS
Nashville, Tennessee

4223-11
ISBN: 0-8054-2311-7

Dewey Decimal Classification: 264
Subject heading: PUBLIC WORSHIP

Library of Congress Catalog Card Number: 81-65390
Printed in the United States of America.

To
Dr. John W. Carlton
Professor about the Word
Spokesman of the Word
Friend in the Word

ACKNOWLEDGMENTS

To my wife who has been a partner, teacher, and an enabler in my leadership in worship and my writing;

To my children who have encouraged my continued creativity in worship;

To the minister and minister of education of my seminary church, Dr. John R. Claypool and Dr. G. Temp Sparkman, Crescent Hill Baptist Church, Louisville, Kentucky, whose innovative approach to worship inspired my searching and my growth in this area;

To many preachers who knowingly and unknowingly have contributed to my understanding of worship—some have inspired me because they were good and some because they were so poor;

To my faithful former secretary and loyal friend, Brenda Ramsey, who assisted immeasurably with the typing;

To those congregations who have responded affirmatively to creative helps in authentic worship: Temple Baptist Church, Durham, North Carolina and First Baptist Church, Concord, North Carolina;

To my present company of worshipers, Southside Baptist Church, Birmingham, Alabama, who, through their encouragement, receptivity, and support, call forth my creative gifts in designing weekly *New Forms of Christian Worship* to enable our encounter with God to be fresh and transforming.

Preface

Two decades ago I began serving a church in rural Virginia as a Sunday pastor. There were disadvantages for the church and for me in this union of struggling church and college student. However, there were many rich experiences that far outweighed the negative factors. Among the many realities I early encountered was the stark fact that I had to plan worship every week! I had no training and little experience in designing worship, and thus I began a quest that is not yet completed. Indeed, the quest of preparing meaningful experiences of worship is one I will continue until I retire.

This book is designed to aid the lay worship committee and the minister who seek to understand worship more completely and to prepare for worship in a more thorough and exciting manner. Contrary to what some may feel or say, worship that is prepared need not be cold or stilted. In fact planned worship can be the most stimulating and rewarding worship experiences one can encounter.

Part I provides a basic backdrop for grasping what worship is and how the congregation can become involved in worship. The first chapter offers a historical/theological definition of worship. The second chapter spills out of the research and experiments related to my doctoral dissertation in which I determined ways to enhance lay perception through increased lay participation in the worship event. Chapter 3 breaks down the basic ingredients of worship so the reader can perceive the breadth and depth of what is involved in the worship experience.

Part II offers the vital aspect for stimulating worship—planning! Exciting worship that covers the scope of the needs of the worshipers and the events of the Christian Year must be thought through and anticipated well in advance. After drawing up the basic design for a year, careful planning must be involved in the planning of weekly worship.

Part III suggests some means for staying in touch with how the worshipers are appreciating what is being done in worship. Some approaches for evaluation are provided in the first chapter. The second chapter offers some sample evaluations to use or modify.

Part IV gives the guidelines and inspiration for planning worship on some of the key special days of the year. Each chapter includes the order of worship for that day, along with some key factors to bear in mind in planning the worship.

The book concludes with a forthright challenge to be excited and prepared in the celebration of worship in church. Although there are many distractions to worship and many who feel that corporate worship is going out of style, understanding and faithful work can provide stimulating encounters with God in church!

Contents

Part I
Understanding Worship

We give God the supreme worth in our lives when we worship him. The psalmist said we are to "give unto the Lord the glory due his name" (29:2). The worship event confronts us with the gospel of Jesus Christ and all its calming comfort and imperative claims. Genuine worship stirs our hearts, stimulates our minds, and motivates our feet for Christian living.

The Sunday morning worship hour is an American tradition. This fact does not reflect the significance of worship for the majority of people. Actually, for many it is more of an indication of their religious habits because vast numbers of churches are lacking in their understanding of the dynamics of worship.

The call for renewal in the church is being sounded within the mainline denominations. Most renewal groups focus their efforts on lay renewal, baptism of the Holy Spirit, or prayer groups. Few recognize the vital aspect of worship. Few identify the urgent need of worship's renewal. Few emphasize the crucial truth that Christianity will die without living encounters with the one true God.

A concept of worship that is not understood cannot be enacted. This first portion of the book focuses on the need for and potential of understanding worship in such a manner that it will become an uplifting, stimulating encounter between the worshipers and God. Separate chapters are devoted to the biblical theory of what worship is, who the worshipers are, and what comprises the various elements of worship. The thesis of this section is not to enable people to worship God as they please on their own terms but to worship God as he pleases to reveal himself through his Word.

1
What Is Worship?

Worship involves all of life and a specific act in a definite place. Christian worship is not authentic without a specific encounter with God that produces definite obedience to God. Worship is a response to God's revelation in Christ. Worship is inspired by gratitude and rooted in the historical Christian heritage. Worship is an experience in which worshipers need guidance and time to speak and listen. Worship is a giving to and a receiving from God. Worship affects one's thoughts and one's feelings, necessitating a clear head and a warm heart. Indeed, worship involves the whole person! The religious emotions of worship include wonder, gratitude, fear, reverence, and baffling mystery. Corporate worship is a congregational event. However, it often degenerates into nothing more than performance alternating between the minister and choir.[1]

Sunday morning worship has been termed by some as the deadest hour of the week. Many people get up on Sunday morning out of habit and sit half-conscious for an hour, passively reacting to what takes place. One of the century's leading thinkers, Karl Barth, is credited with saying that Christians go to church to make their last stand—*against* God! Instead of a time to encounter God, many church members are busy elevating their self-made gods while they are in the sanctuary. Some have seen worship as show business—cheap show business since one neither has to pay nor often feels he sees good performance. The overarching attitude toward God tends to be a struggle and indifference instead of submission and commitment.

Many community-minded, church-renewal people have been

guilty of downgrading the real value of worship. The emphasis is more on doing for God rather than hearing what God intends for his people to do. For a long time children of the church have been told that entering the sanctuary is going to "big church." Sunday School members on a six-point record system have been asked if they were going to "stay for preaching service." Many have come to think this single hour a week constitutes their "Christian service." Preaching is downplayed by those who say they do not want anyone to preach at them. What they mean is they do not want anyone to say anything negative or hateful to them.

One night Snuffy Smith was fitful and could not sleep. When he was dressed and about to go out for a walk, Aunt Loweezy reminded him how dangerous it was to venture out in the dark with the wild animals, neighbors who might shoot at him, a creek he might fall into, or a cold he might take. By the time she had run the list of nighttime drawbacks, Snuffy was sound asleep. She carried him off to bed, saying that all he needed for good sleep was an old-fashioned sermon! Culture has implied this hour is just "preaching," when in fact, preaching occupies less than two-fifths of the hour of worship.

Without question, bad taste in the church's approach to worship takes its toll on people—like the church that advertises its Sunday worship as "The Pause that Refreshes" or the one that invites the public with the words, "Why Not Try God?" Worship is defective and nonbiblical when it is so flat and sweet. It is not Christian, when the language is not artistic and beautiful, and when it is unfaithful to God as revealed in Jesus Christ. Worship is defective in form, function, and substance when it is designed only to fit the leader's motives and plans. One writer described Sunday morning in some churches:

Once inside the church a visitor is enjoined, "Please wear a red bow and fill out the guest card," as eager "greeters" roll him into the hands of an aggressive usher who ostentatiously leads him to a seat, handing him a garish bulletin with smudged mimeographing bearing

at the top the cliché: "Enter to worship, go forth to serve." The
congregation engages in a buzz of conversational small talk while the
organist competes for attention playing Liszt's "Liebestraum." The
choir, wearing green vestments with taupe stoles, enters on the opening hymn in hesitation-waltz step. The minister, clad in black gown
with academic hood, conspicuously takes up a position as master of
ceremonies, and fetches out of his hip pocket a hand edition of the
New Testament from which he will presently read a few verses as
springboard for his climatic "message," preparing himself from time
to time with a draught from a prominent glass of water. The opening
invocation becomes a sermon with everyone's eyes closed, and the
"responsive reading" which follows, with the congregation sitting,
concludes with the solo, "The Holy City." Two hymns follow, concluding what is labelled on the bulletin as "I-Preparation." The
service then proceeds with the offering, prefaces with an urging to
present "folded money that will make Jesus smile," and the collection
plates are retained at the rear of the auditorium while the ushers count
the money as the minister's "morning prayer" wanders from home-
town to the communists and back again. Next follows a long and
pretentious anthem which stalls all movement, and the service grinds
to a temporary halt. After the sermon and recessional, the benediction—laced with sentiments of the preacher's contriving—is pro-
nounced from the rear of the church, and immediately after an
"Amen" *a la* Richard Wagner, organ chimes sound "God Be With
You Till We Meet Again." The service ends with a mounting cre-
scendo of conversation competing with fortissimo organ postlude.[2]

We live in a land where our ancestors gave their lives in order
that we might have freedom to worship God together as he
leads us. Two centuries later, less than two out of five Americans worship God. The Christian church is somewhat like the
experience one little girl related. She asked her mother if she
remembered the old vase that had been handed down from generation to generation in her family. When the mother replied
she knew the vase, the daughter responded that she was sorry
but the new generation had dropped it! Children and young
adults alike often mirror the religious attitudes and practices of

their parents. Dropping corporate worship from one's life is frequently learned in the home.

A boy arrived late for the morning worship. He slipped in near the back of the sanctuary. After worship, the minister greeted the boy and asked why he was late. The lad stared at the floor for a moment and then said he was about to go fishing, but his dad would not let him go. Though surprised the boy would consider going fishing on Sunday, the minister congratulated the wisdom of the boy's father. He asked if the father had explained why the boy could not go. The little fellow quickly answered: "He said there wasn't enough bait for both of us to go fishing, so he went alone."

Before you rule out the meaning and vitality of regular, weekly, corporate worship, take a close look at some crucial aspects of worship. Worship, simply put, is the acknowledgment of God's supreme worth. We worship God because of who he is, not because of what he can do for us. We worship not to glorify ourselves but to celebrate God's majesty. We do not worship to build up our church, its program, or even God's kingdom. We worship to affirm what God has done, what God is doing, and what God will do. Contrary to what some may believe or say, worship is an obligation not an option for the Christian. Worship is not always easy. It always requires disciplined effort.

To worship is to quicken the conscience of the holiness of God, to feed the mind with the truth of God, to purge the imagination by the beauty of God, to open the heart to the love of God, to devote the will to the purpose of God. All this is gathered up in that emotion which most cleanses us from selfishness because it is the most selfless of all emotions—adoration.[5]

Worship is directed toward God not any person or organization. We honor *God.* We praise *God.* We adore *God.* We obey *God.* We praise *God* above all the earth. The psalmist was marvelous at expressing joy and praise before God. Psalm 95

instructs God's people to praise God, to be joyful, to give
thanks, and to be humble.

Through worship we gain a vision of God. We interpret life
and work under God, and we dedicate life to God. We give our
tribute to God in worship, acknowledging his holiness and
providence. In worship, we remember God's mighty acts in our
behalf, affirm our faith, and celebrate God's grace in making
us persons of worth, able to come before him. People who have
no real feelings of self-worth cannot or will not worship God.
They will seek to use God like they use people—to make themselves feel good. In Jesus Christ, God offers us self-esteem and
self-worth.

Worship provides the occasion for seeking restitution to God
through confessing our sins, asking and receiving forgiveness,
and dedicating ourselves afresh to him. Humility is very defi-
nitely involved in worship, though humility may become pretentious and false. We have rightly perceived the publican in the
Gospels as a righteous man because he humbly prayed before
God to be merciful to him, a sinner. However, if that is *all* we
ever do—just dwell on our human sinfulness and our human
limitations—we experience no change at the powerful and loving hand of God! Week after week we ask only for mercy and
refuse transformation and redemption!

Worship also offers the opportunity for us to experience rich
communion with God and with others. God created us to know
the rhythm of work and rest, labor and relaxation, stress and
release, sound and silence. We must learn under God how to
integrate genuine worship into our complex, busy lives. We
must learn that worship should be descriptive of our total life
experience. Worship is no more confined to the sanctuary than
our religious expressions in life are confined to the worship
room. We worship corporately in the sanctuary so that we
might worship better in all that we do the rest of the week in the
world. When we worship, the drudgery is taken out of life.
When we are in tune with our Maker, all of life is full of joy

and meaning. Without worship, our purpose and direction for living are lacking. We are out of step with God and with ourselves. We have all experienced the frustration of seeing a film in which the mouth and body movements of the actors were not synchronized. This is a mental picture of what takes place in our lives when we are living apart from a regular, genuine worship experience with God.

The story is told of a city in Europe that was shelled a great deal in World War I without experiencing much damage. The account states:

A shell ran alongside one street through the top floor of one house (and the inhabitants were in the kitchen), then through the bottom story of the next (and the inhabitants were on the landing above), and finally settled, unexploded, somewhere in the third.

Most of the shells did not explode because, being meant to impact against the hard steel of battleships, the walls of the . . . houses were too *soft* for them.[4]

The lives of many church members have never beeen stirred by the presence and movement of the Almighty God because their minds are theologically so woolly and soft there is nothing for God's Word or God's presence to strike and lodge in! We have missed the point when we think that a single hour is the "worship service" of the Christian's week. We are wrong to conceive of an hour on Sunday morning as all of the worship we are to give God. We are wrong to think that encountering God in worship constitutes our Christian service. When corporate worship occurs in a genuine, personal, authentic manner, we will be prepared to worship God in each experience every day of the week. When true worship takes place on Sunday morning, we will be inspired to serve God daily through every opportunity we have. The sanctuary is not a filling station where we are to sit passively waiting to view a performance, to receive some blessing, or to see and hear what is available. Worship is an act! We are to give ourselves to God, tell God of our love and admiration for him, and lay ourselves open to his majesty.

Our worship is to be directed toward God if it is divine worship. Our Almighty God is the One who can give the power and direction to bring our out-of-sync movements and speech back together. Our worship is not to have an ulterior motive of what we can get for ourselves or even for the church to which we belong. Our worship is to be our sheer gift of ourselves to God. What takes place as a result of our worship is a benefit of God's continuing gift to us.

John wrote in Revelation 19 what the praise of God would be like in heaven. He wrote that the leaders worshiped God saying, "Amen. Alleluia!" (v. 4). These are two simple and rather common words in our vocabulary, but they are powerful in directing our attention to what worship is truly intended to be. *Amen* in Greek literally means "so let it be" or "so be it Lord." A Christian uses the word to simultaneously express the joy of knowing God through salvation in Christ and the assurance of being possessed by and belonging to Christ. Saying "so let it be" to God involves a submission to accept the will of God and to commit oneself to the purpose of God. Saying "amen" means that we are putting ourselves at God's disposal as our ultimate offering to him. Jesus spoke of worshiping in spirit and truth (John 4). That involves offering ourselves in the ultimate, complete sense to God!

Alleluia is a Greek word which translates the Hebrew word meaning "Praise Yahweh" or "Praise God." Alleluia is the aspect of worship that recaptures the awareness that in God's presence is joy and at his right hand are pleasures forevermore! And as we know joy in the fellowship of God, so we experience assurance of the victory of God through genuine worship. In spite of the seeming defeat of Christ, God demonstrated through the empty tomb that he will not be overcome. In spite of our struggles, pain, hurt, and seeming defeat, God assures us we will not be overcome when we know, love, and worship him.

We are going to worship someone or something. We are created by God with the desire to worship him. If that desire is unfulfilled, we will worship something in his place. We basically worship what is most sacred to us—what we hold in the highest esteem, what we revere, what we give our ultimate loyalty to. Martin Luther said our god is whatever we would sacrifice our daughters for—be that our work, our homes, our travel, our pleasure, our possessions, or our country. If we do not worship God, we will find or make another god, or else we will wind up worshiping ourselves.

A "Star Trek" story told of a winged serpent who considered himself to be a god. He treated people as children he could lead around and who would worship him. He became very upset when people forgot about him. His encounter with the *Enterprise* crew enabled them to see that he was not a god, for this being lacked power, knowledge, and kindness that God possesses. This being was nothing more than an egotistical maniac who wanted people to worship him. This story only tends to underscore our tendency as human beings. Either we resort to egotistical mania in order to have people worship us or we find some other object or person to whom we can give our ultimate loyalty and worship. We will not rest until we are worshiping. The sad reality is our worship will never give us contentment until we are worshiping the one true and living God!

Worship is more than feeling. Worship is more than thought. Worship involves the total person. Many who have found worship to be uninspiring have made the mistake of using just their feelings or just their thoughts. We will never know authentic worship until we avoid the two extremes and use all of the capabilities God has given us to worship him in spirit and truth with heart and mind. It is hard for us to focus on the primary need of life—to worship God—when we are so swamped with the common, ordinary, secondary things.

This very fact of our weakness in worship is why corporate worship is so vital. While all of our worship is not confined to the sanctuary when we are together with other Christians, the Bible teaches that worship *is* a community affair with God and with others. Unless we worship properly in the sanctuary, we will not worship properly alone. Likewise, private worship apart from corporate worship is necessary for worship in the sanctuary to be complete. Once a minister was approached by a young man who asked if he should come to worship when he did not want to come. He said sometimes he enjoyed the experience, but other times he had no desire. He questioned if it would not be hypocritical for him to come when his desire for worship was not great. The wise minister replied:

Do you only pay the grocer's bill and the rent when you feel like it? Worship is a debt to be discharged independently of our feelings; it is giving unto the Lord the glory DUE unto His name; hence "it is obligatory on Christians." The primary purpose of worship is the glory of God, not the edification of man.[5]

Unless we rightly worship God, we will neither learn of God nor of ourselves.

The Greek word for *worship* is also translated "service." That does not mean we can call the worship hour the "worship service" and claim to have fulfilled both needs. It is to say that worship and service are required of us when we acknowledge God as our God. Worship becomes the essence of life when we worship God fully in the sanctuary and continue to worship him in the world as we are also serving him. Paul gave the biblical concept of worship in 1 Corinthians when he said that worship is basically corporate and strengthens the body of believers. Indeed, if a religious community does not worship, it is not Christian. And if worship does not undergird and uplift the community, it is not Christian worship!

Christian worship is never solitary for long. As is reflected in the Lord's Prayer, worship has a vital corporate aspect to it. The pronouns used are the plural "our," "we," and "us"; not the singular "I." People can sit by their televisions all they want and receive some inspiration from religious programming, but genuine worship requires an on-going community dimension. Such worship saves us from religious egotism and frees us for selfless living. Corporate worship provides the orientation for all of life to be dedicated into God's hands and leading. Once a deaf-mute person was asked why he came to worship each Sunday when he could not hear what was being said. He wrote quickly his answer: "I come each week to let people know which side I am on."[6] Thus corporate worship allows us the unique opportunity to adore God while declaring to others that he is our God. On the basis of this experience, we are more capable of showing forth that he is God the other six days of the week. Worship is "the total adoring response of man to the one Eternal God self-revealed in time."[7]

Merely worshiping is not enough. We have to be thoughtful and careful that we worship the one true and living God and not some leader, some movement, some organization, some church, or even some nation. Not long ago a leading Baptist declared :

We stand with goose pimples running up and down our backs, and pledge allegiance to the flag and "America under God," or we like to hear Kate Smith belt out "God Bless America" and feel that this is a token acknowledgement of the true living God to save our national conscience. . . . In taking the nation as a whole, I see us taking false gods which is the sin most paramount in the national culture to-day. . . . We have bowed down and worshiped the gods of material-ism, the gods of prestige, gods of power, gods of possession.[8]

The object of our worship is crucial. True worship is our obli-gation, not our choice, if we know Christ as our Lord! God made us and has redeemed us; we owe him our loyalty, alle-giance, and awe!

We worship God not for what we will benefit but because of who he is and what he has done for us. However, when we wor-ship in spirit and in truth, we are renewed by worship just as the body is renewed by sleep. We grow in Christ only when we truly worship in Christ. Failure to worship is like wearing glasses

behind which there are no eyes! Worship that transforms life
was witnessed in Berlin not many years ago. A church's prop-
erty was divided by the iron curtain. The church building was
left in East Berlin and the parsonage in West Berlin. The church
youth in the West decided to gather in the parsonage on Reformation Sunday and sing Luther's great hymn, "A Mighty Fortress Is Our God." They hoped their Christian brothers on the
other side of the wall might hear them and be uplifted by their
encouragement to trust in and worship God also. The Christian
youth in the Communist sector gathered at the same time. Just
before Luther's hymn was begun, the Christians in East Berlin
began to sing an old Reformation hymn they revived after a
century of no use. They sang:

> I can't go on.
> No comfort here abideth,
> Life's burden weighs me down
> It is too much!
> I cannot find relief
> All comfort takes its leave!
> Have mercy on me, Lord!
> I can't go on!

Quickly the Western youth changed hymns and responded with
the second verse of the same hymn:

> You can go on!
> God's help will soon be there.
> He'll turn you from your grief
> And give you peace.
> You just must keep on fighting.
> Our Lord too suffered in His stride.
> Go on with Him—He's on your side.
> You can go on!

The youth in the East sang the third stanza about their inability
to go on, and then the youth on both sides of the wall, topped
with barbed wire and broken glass, sang the final stanza:

You can go on!
There soon will be an end.
God reaches out His hand,
Look here—His hand, to you!
Ah, let us pray and pray.
And He will send the day.
His help will make us say,
To Him be praise,
He is our strength and stay.[9]

This is worship at its best—the prayer to and praise of the Almighty God that fills us with joy at who he is and transforms us into a living fellowship with him in the very essence of life. When we worship ourselves or some other false gods, there is no strength to go on. But when we are willing to worship the true and living God, we can go on, we can go on!

Worship at its best is enabling the worshipers to find the resources to go on in life, to go on in their spiritual pilgrimage in the power and the presence of the unseen Father.

Notes

1. Stephen F. Winward, *The Reformation of Our Worship* (Richmond, Va.: John Knox Press, 1965), pp. 1 8.

2. From *The Integrity of Worship* by Paul W. Hoon. Copyright ©1971 Abingdon Press. Used by permission, pp. 38-39.

3. William Temple, *The Hope of a New World* (New York: The Macmillan Company, Ltd., 1942), p. 30

4. Thomas H. Keh, *The Word in Worship* (New York: Oxford University Press, 1962), p. 15.

5. Daniel D. Walker, *Enemy in the Pew?* (New York: Harper and Row, Publishers, 1967), p. 60.

6. Ibid., p. 72.

7. Evelyn Underhill, *Worship* (New York: Harper and Row, Publishers, 1957), p. 61.

8. Mark Hatfield, *The Religious Herald* (Richmond, Va., January 17, 1974), p. 21.

9. Walker, pp. 68-69.

2
Looking at the Worshipers

A cartoon pictured a man kneeling, proposing to a woman. She questioned him about their religious differences because she worshiped money and he was broke! It is imperative to determine what worship is and who the object of worship is. A further step to take is to recognize who the worshipers are.

Kierkegaard's analogy of the play most aptly portrays the biblical concept of worshipers. Worship is a two-way event in which we are directly involved with God, as he is with us. For every actor who strides onto center stage, there is a prompter in the wings ready to help should the actor hesitate or forget. In worship, the people at the front—the preacher, choir, and other worship leaders—are not the actors; the congregation is! The people gathered in the worship room are not an audience observing a performance; God is! All assembled in God's sanctuary are involved in the active drama of worshiping God who is the only One observing what is done. The role of the worship leaders is to aid and prompt an active encounter with God on the part of all the people.

Many things get in the way of the worshipers and God. We are distracted by what was left cooking at home and by what must be cooked when we get home. We are distracted by the gnawing of unconfessed sin, by the alienation of being at odds with another worshiper, or by the emptiness of bearing a grudge. We are distracted by the loneliness caused by being out of tune with God. We are distracted by being strangers in the congregation. We are distracted by sadness—grief, sorrow, disillusionment, doubt, and pain inflicted by others. We are distracted by the people who are present and by the people who are absent, by those who lead the worship and by the sins of others in the congregation. We are distracted by the pains and problems of the world, as well as by our own pains and problems.

Worshipers come in all shapes, sizes, ages, and backgrounds. Some are young Christians, and some have been in the faith for a half-century or more. Some have been accustomed to worshiping in one congregation all their lives, and others have come to that place only in recent weeks or months. Some come with preparation and anticipation for worship, and others are merely present in body. There is a divided response in worship, just as John reminded us (John 12:29). When a heavenly voice affirmed Jesus' declaration of his mission, some said it thundered while others said an angel spoke. The background and reputation of worshipers is varied and the leader must take this factor into account.

A Texas pastor related the experience of being invited to lunch at the home of a church family right at the peak of the harvest season. In that part of the country, neighboring farmers helped one another at harvesttime. The farmers' wives had spent the morning preparing a nourishing country meal. Five minutes before twelve the host's younger son rang the dinner bell. Within minutes nearly twenty hungry men came in to wash their faces and hands and gather about the long table. They came with a sense of joy, excitement, and anticipation. The pastor realized the only blessing that would be appreciated would be a brief one, for these men had come to eat! With the "amen," the men ate with such freedom and delight that the pastor found himself enjoying watching the men eat more that he was enjoying his own food! They ate and laughed and laughed and ate.

When the food had been consumed, the men returned to their harvesting. The pastor drove back to the small town where the church building was located. As he approached the building, he saw the spire and bell tower. Then he remembered the dinner bell. He thought about how the people in the town and surrounding countryside would respond to the ringing of that church bell on Sunday morning. Most of them would come without a sense of enthusiasm or joy. They would not have the same attitude which he had just seen exhibited by those farmers coming in response to the dinner bell. He asked himself what the difference was. One answer he discovered was that the church members would not have been working faithfully in the Master's fields. Only those who have been laboring in the Master's harvest were eager to come to the Master's table! Only after we respond to God's call to work in his harvest will the church bells sound as attractive as the dinner bells, calling us to celebrate the Lord of the harvest and to renew our strength for the harvest.

Frequently worshipers are ignored by those who plan and lead the worship. Every faithful homemaker has the same goal of preparing nourishing food for her family. In various parts of the country, the menu varies and the food is seasoned differently. Those responsible for designing the worship experience must not do so in oblivion to the background and needs of the people who will gather for worship in that particular place on a specific Sunday.

Many seminaries and divinity schools have trained ministers in the last half of this century to feel that the most important role they had was to do one-on-one pastoral counseling. Indeed, some seminary graduates have tended to look down upon their peers who were not sharp enough or thoughtful enough to turn their careers toward clinical pastoral care and instead went into the local church ministry. Surely the counseling role of the minister is not to be belittled, but there is another dimension to the function of a Christian minister.

During the Protestant Reformation, a break was made with the priestly role of the minister. The pastoral role became the focal point and the priestly functions were either degraded or overlooked. This historical movement has caused us to come to this day with the healing, reconciling, and sustaining work of the Christian minister largely removed from the community life. This vital work of the minister has become isolated in one-to-one individualistic, psychologically permeated settings, frequently with little theological orientation or connection with the corporate community.

Pastoral care is frequently sought by people who desire to understand themselves through a theological perspective. The worshiping community can provide both the beginning and the context for such pastoral care. Unfortunately too many ministers hear only the psychological and not the theological/faith needs of their members. Pastoral care is not the reason for worship, but it is certainly an outgrowth of genuine divine worship. Indeed, it is difficult to sustain authentic pastoral care apart from corporate worship.[1]

Bearing in mind who the worshipers are will prevent the worship event from being conceived of as an ivory-tower experience, divorced from the world. Allowing the pastoral encounters outside the sanctuary to inform the minister of the people's needs will enable him to structure a worship encounter in which God and the worshipers can interact at the very point of pain or joy in the worshipers' lives.

The worship leader will enhance the flow of worship when he remembers that he is not giving a performance for people to observe. He is not a showman and the congregation is not the audience. Just as real worship is a two-way encounter between God and man, so the event of worship is a two-way dialogue between the congregation and the worship leader. The worshipers will be encouraged to take a more active part in worship when they sense everyone in the worship room is involved in worship and that the worship leaders are just that—leaders! The worship leaders, particularly the preacher for the day, will be enlightened by observing the facial feedback of the worshipers. Indeed, the congregation needs to be informed that the preaching minister will be looking for their involvement in the preaching event in order to determine whether his point is being heard and understood. Attentiveness is part of the feedback. But even more, a smile at a pun, a laugh at humor, a pensive face at a thorny issue, or a troubled face at a compassionate moment will tell the speaker that he is being heard—with meaning!

Worshipers who are taught they have a theological reason for being as involved in worship as the worship leader need to be provided the opportunity for direct involvement in ways other than singing and listening. While the next chapter will go into detail in this matter, the point must be clearly understood that there are numerous helpful ways of involving the people in the worship event. And there is documentary evidence to underscore the fact that when people are involved in worship, they understand and retain more of what transpires in the worship event.[2]

The role of the worshiper can be elevated if each Sunday each worshiper has the opportunity to speak by participating in a corporate reading of some type. This speaking may be in the form of

- a unison Scripture reading
- a responsive call to worship
- a corporate offertory response
- a unison summons to worship
- a responsive Scripture reading
- a corporate statement of belief
- a unison benediction
- a responsive offertory prayer
- a litany of thanksgiving
- a corporate summons to prayer
- a responsive benediction
- a corporate invocation
- a unison statement of faith.

The possibilities are numerous. The important factor to bear in mind is that the spoken statement on the part of the worshiper does several things. For one, it reminds him that the worship leader takes seriously the worshiper's need for direct involvement. His attention is heightened. His dignity is affirmed. His self-worth before God is increased. In the second place, a spoken role allows the worshiper to express something of himself. If he is not living up to what he is asked to say, he is learning what Christian discipleship does involve and thus raises his goal of worship and living. Hearing the community of believers say the same thing at the same time is encouraging to the one who is seeking to maintain a close relationship with God, just as it inspires those out of tune with God to draw nigh to him. Thirdly, speaking is an active participation in worship. It says to the worshiper that he is not a passive spectator. It also teaches the worshiper that worship is an act, an offering of self; he is given the opportunity to participate in such an offering of himself.

The worshipers can be involved in worship musically in ways other than the standard hymns. A corporate musical call to worship, singing the Lord's Prayer for the invocation or benediction, a corporate musical meditation or call to prayer, and a congregational musical offertory response are just some of the ways to enable the entire congregation to increase their activity in worship through music. Additional choirs other than the adult choir can be trained and used to lead worship, adding direct involvement on the part of the choir members and further inspiration for the worshipers who hear the music. Handbell choirs, instrumentalists, as well as instrumental ensembles, can be incorporated into the worship experience. This would enable musicians from within the congregation as well as guest musicians to lead in worship.

The worship leaders must bear in mind that worship does initiate some resistance as well as positive response. People desire to conceal as well as to reveal, to protect as well as to project.[3] Resistance may be employed by worshipers in order to protect themselves from overwhelming truths encountered in worship. This is not all bad, contrary to what church leaders have been accustomed to thinking. Instead of resistance being equated with failure on the part of leaders, worship, or the church in general, resistance can be interpreted as indicative that the church is about its business! Resistance can provide an opportunity for ministry, a handle for understanding and dealing with feelings and concerns of worshipers. Resistance may well be a part of worship, for in coming face-to-face with the Almighty God there may be some unpleasant, discomforting, and unnerving experiences from which you wish to flee! But it is at the point of uneasy resistance that the minister can determine what healing needs to occur for the worshipers.

The worshiper is an important person in the sight of God, a vision that will be illumined when he feels he is important to the minister and worship leaders. The worshiper is involved in a unique, corporate, divine-human drama in which he is the chief actor and God the sole audience. The manner in which he worships indicates the God or god whom he worships. In the past, most of the blame has been cast at the worshipers' feet for the lack of inspiring, uplifting responsiveness in worship. Now we can recognize that the worship leadership has a significant responsibility in the worship event. The Christian worshiper still has definite obligations. Perhaps these "Ten Commandments of Worship," found in an old English church, sum up the "manners" that will encourage better worship on the part of the worshiping community.

1. Thou shalt not come to service late,
   Nor for the amen refuse to wait.
2. When speaks the organ's sweet refrain,
   The noisy tongue shalt thou restrain.
3. But when the hymns are sounded out,
   Thou shalt lift thy voice and shout.
4. And when the anthem thou shalt hear,
   Thy sticky voice thou shalt not clear.

5. The endmost seat thou shalt leave free,
   For more must share the pew with thee.
6. The offering plate thou shalt not fear,
   But give thine utmost with cheer.
7. Thou shalt the minister give heed,
   Nor blame him when thou art disagreed.
8. Unto thy neighbor thou shalt bend,
   And if a stranger, make a friend.
9. Thou shalt in every way be compassionate,
   kind, considerate, and tender-minded.
10. And so be all thy spirit's grace,
    Thou shalt show God within this place.

The worshiper is not a passive spectator who comes looking for what he can see, get, hear, or receive. The worshiper is an active participant in an encounter with God, an encounter of giving, telling, and acting in the presence of the Almighty God! The worshiper is interested in vitality, freshness, variety, precision, enlightenment, and joy in worship. Anything less than this is a discredit to the Caller who calls all of us to worship him and calls out leaders to enable others to worship.

Notes

1. William H. Willimon, *Worship as Pastoral Care* (New York: Abingdon Press, 1979), pp. 35-41.

2. Robert W. Bailey, "The Revitalization of the Preaching Event With Emphasis Upon Lay Participation and Perception," Unpublished S.T.D. Dissertation, The Southern Baptist Theological Seminary, Louisville, Kentucky, 1970.

3 Willimon, pp. 75 f.

3
The Components of Worship

Worship has been misconceived by both the minister and the congregation—sometimes alike and sometimes quite differently. The minister may feel it is "the preaching service." The people on both sides of the pulpit may come to the worship room unprepared, and they may fail to find the ingredients necessary to facilitate and enable the worship experience once they have gathered.

Being present for the hour of worship does not necessarily mean a person has worshiped God. Worship involves praise, adoration, and an awareness of God. Worship also involves humility, confession, and forgiveness. Contemplation, offering, thanksgiving, proclamation, dedication, and commitment are all part of worship. Overlooking the components of worship negates the true power and meaning of worship at the outset. The absence of reverence and anticipation on the part of the congregation and worship leaders prior to and during the worship experience distract from the potential experience of worship. Loud speech, laughing, and casual visiting are not appropriate responses of reverence on the part of the worshipers. Neither is joking, talking back and forth, entering late, or making loud noises prior to entering appropriate for the worship leaders—minister and musicians.

The five to fifteen minutes prior to the worship hour are important in terms of setting the mood for the worship experience. Some unusual components of worship may be explained or even practiced during these minutes when most of the congregation has gathered. Music can be of vital importance during this time. The organ, piano, handbells, and other instruments can be effectively used to draw the worshipers' minds away from the mundane distractions into holy awe of God's presence. This music needs to be well planned and well rehearsed in order to achieve such a high purpose. It also needs to begin prior to the stated hour for the spoken worship to begin.

Frequently choral meditations or chorales may be used for pre-worship music. In each instance, the precision and feeling of the music plays a vital role in the attitude of the worshipers. Loud, boisterous music will only be outtalked by the congregation. Soft, unrehearsed, ill-planned music will be ignored. Proper music to inspire the worship of God done to the best of the musicians' ability will invoke a spirit of proper worship.

Music is not an afterthought or a cover-up of the transitions in worship. A visitor in Germany once asked a local townsman where he might hear the most interesting music. The German replied they did not have any music in church. Surprised, the stranger asked if they sang no hymns. The townsman quickly responded that they did—but they did not consider that listening to music, that was worship! It was in such an atmosphere of church music that Bach grew up and later said, "All music should have no other end and aim than the glory of God and the re-creation of the soul."

More worshipers learn their views of God from music than from sermons. For this reason, hymns and anthems should be selected only after careful examination of their wording. Sometimes careful scrutiny necessitates the elimination of an "old favorite" and "an exciting new song" alike. Music can be an asset to basically every facet of worship. Thus, it needs to be theologically sound and heartily and accurately rendered.

A vital, initial component of worship is that of praising and adoring God. The early Christian church had four basic ingredients in their worship—praise, prayer, proclamation, and offering. We cannot worship rightly until we recapture, as the principle element in worship, the overwhelming sense of awe and reverence in the presence of God. God's greatness, love, and compassion call forth our praise and adoration. The sad reality is that God's presence is not even acknowledged by some who gather in the worship room. The unfortunate merger of church programs (man-centered) with worship (God-centered) has created the cloudy thinking in the minds of many. Rather than entering into a unique setting of God's presence in order to praise and glorify him, numerous persons come to support a leader, "pack a pew," hear the music, enjoy a special promotion, or hear an inspiring sermon. Worship is not man-centered. Worship is God-centered! Therefore, worship must include, at the outset, the element of praise and adoration so that the worshipers might once again get in tune with the presence of God.

Prayer is a vital aspect of worship. Few worship hours include less than four prayers, and some have as many as seven or eight. Frequently there is little distinction between the various prayers, nor is there much variation between prayers from one Sunday to the next. Prayer is an opportunity of intercession with God—a time of acknowledging his presence and seeking his leadership. Prayer is a time of expressing humility before him, making confession of sins, asking forgiveness for sins. Through prayer, we offer ourselves to God, petition for daily needs, thank God for blessings, and interceding for others. Prayer is a way of expressing renewed dedication to God.

Prayer is not one man talking to another. Prayer is profound conversation with God. Corporate prayer is not an attempt to impress with oratorical skills or Elizabethan mastery. Corporate prayer is interaction with God under the leadership of one person. The prayer of the leader is the direction and inspiration for the individual worshipers to respond to God in prayer.

Prayer is not completed with the speaking of the pray-er. Prayer is completed only when those praying listen to God. Of vital importance is the incorporation of the element of silence into the worship experience. Some people are very uncomfortable with silence. Some worshipers will cough or squirm, and some musicians will play in order to avoid the deafening sounds of silence. Effective worship can be achieved when the worshipers are led to learn how to understand, appreciate, and use silence for rich communion with God.

The reading of the Bible is a central component in worship. Scripture passages that are poorly read are great distractions to the hearing and heeding of God's Word. A lack of variety in Scripture reading also detracts from the power and meaning of the sixty-six separate writings that make up the Bible. Preaching that is divorced from or not well grounded in accurate reading and interpretation of the Bible amounts to little more than the whims and concerns of one man. The living Word of God is to be lifted up with clarity and precision—not in an attempt to have the people worship the Bible but in order that the people might once again hear what has taken place between God and his people, and thus be prepared to interact with God in that very hour. A vision of God is difficult to gain apart from a live understanding of the Word of God. Worship necessitates careful reading of key passages from the Old and New Testaments, using a variety of the best translations. Paraphrases should only be read if a careful exegesis of the Scripture will relate an accurate meaning of the text.

Proclamation of the Word is crucially important. The Scripture verse that is not explained or interpreted may be misunderstood or ignored. Unfortunately, not all so-called "proclamation" is "rightfully dividing the Word of truth!" In the mid 1800s a man was reported to have written: "There is, perhaps, no greater hardship at present inflicted on mankind in civilized and free countries, than the necessity of listening to sermons." There are surely two sides to the reluctance to hear sermons preached. One aspect is that the minister is unprepared to give a fresh, insightful, stimulating interpretation of the present Word God would have heard from the text. The unprepared minister is contemptible for the hearers and demonstrates a lack of reverence for God. The prophet Malachi had a great deal to say to the irreverent priests/proclaimers of his day.[1] For a minister to go into the pulpit unprepared and expect God to give him the words to say impromptu is an unreasonable expectation of God. A minister who goes into the pulpit and offers a cheap gospel and easy grace in order to please the people rather than proclaming the costly price Christ paid and calls all his followers to pay blasphemes against God. The sermon is an offering of the minister to God. If the minister is a man of God, the sermon is to be the minister's best offering for that hour!

A quarter of a century ago a professor of preaching wrote, "If Protestantism ever dies with a dagger in its back, the dagger will be the Protestant sermon."[2] Preaching in the early church was done by those who proclaimed what they had personally experienced at the hand of Christ and the power of the Holy Spirit. Shortly after the apostles' death, preaching fell into decay and, with few exceptions, has continued across the centuries with little sustained enthusiasm or intensity. There is no question that in our nation the minister is no longer the most educated or highly thought of man in the community, and neither is the Sunday sermon the only entertainment option for the week.[3] In spite of all that has been written and said against the sermon in this century, people still long to hear the Word of God accurately and thoroughly interpreted to them with freshness for their day. "Where there is true preaching, where, in the obedience of faith, the Word is proclaimed, there, in spite of all appearances to the contrary, the most important thing that ever happens upon this earth takes place."[4] Many problems block the preaching event from occurring with power and meaning.[5] Part of the problem has to do with how the minister perceives his task. Part has to do with how the worshipers perceive their task. Part of the problem has to do with how the preacher has prepared himself professionally and for that specific sermon. Another problem has to do with how the congregation views their role in the preaching event. Part has to do with the whole context of worship. Part has to do with the language used. Part has to do with the emotions and ideas brought to the worship hour, and part has to do with those emotions and ideas aroused there.

The worship hour is far more than the "preaching service." The minister who has done his homework well will seldom preach more than twenty to twenty-five minutes, which is approximately one-third to two-fifths of the worship hour. The minister who enables the worshipers to feel they are a vital part of what is preached and how it is preached will find a congregation that will inspire and encourage him with their facial feedback during the sermon and with their objective evaluation apart from the worship hour. Preaching that is done with freshness keeps the congregation from feeling they have already heard that before. It will keep the worshipers from erecting their defensive barriers so quickly that they fail to hear what is being said anew that day. Preaching is a powerful event when it is dialogical—involving the hearts and minds of minister and laity alike.

The offering is a central part of worship. Indeed, in the worship of the early church, the offering was the high point of worship. This was the time of thanksgiving to God for all he had done in their creation and in Jesus Christ. This was the time of celebrating what God was doing for and through them. The offering was a specific, deliberate act of worship. It was a means of demonstrating the self-giving of the worshiper to God. It was a joyous time of acknowledging that all one is and has comes as God's gift. The offering, then, is the natural outflow of the life of one who knowingly, willfully belongs to God. The offering is an ongoing reminder of who one belongs to and for whom one is living day by day.

An offering by the worshiper is not essential for God but it is for the worshipers! God will exist without any of us ever giving him another offering. But our relationship of trust, joy, and self-giving will not endure long apart from our regular offering of ourselves, using the tangible material offering as a symbol. The offering is an expression of the obedience of the giver. God is not interested in the mere formality of giving an offering; nor is he concerned about how much tax deduction we receive from our gift. God looks on the heart to see the love and generosity from which the offering comes. Just as Jesus concluded that the wealthy who gave their large sums for show went away estranged from God, so God does not accept a showy or indifferent offering today as a symbol of self-giving. Likewise, as Jesus affirmed the generous, complete self-giving of the widow who gave her all, the contemporary worshiper who allows his offering to express his whole self-giving will enjoy a right relationship to God.

Offering is an act. It is act that every worshiper can enter into. As all of worship is an act, the offering is the central act, the high point of worship—if and when it is done honestly and in the right spirit before God. An offering is a sacrifice. It is the bringing of one's best to God. It is the bringing from "off the top" of one's increase. The biblical offering begins with a tithe of at least 10 percent of one's earnings and then continues as one gives of himself beyond what God has initially required. An offering is a sacrifice of one's means, for the worshiper does have to discipline himself to give it and learn to live without it. An offering is also a sacrifice of one's life, for the true worshiper sees it as an expression of love and self-giving to God, to be used to glorify the name and love of God across the face of the earth.

Unfortunately many have not seen the offering in its theological context. Indeed, ministers and lay leaders alike have commonly referred to the offering as "the collection." Some churches stress taking up the collection during Sunday School. Thus, the worshipers come to the worship hour with no offerings to give. Again, there are leaders and congregations who are so money and budget conscious that they choose to have the money counted during the worship hour, and sometimes even reported to the congregation before worship is concluded! At least two things happen when the money is taken from the sanctuary and counted during the worship hour. One, counters are not involved in worship. Their sole purpose in coming to God's house is to handle the money that will hopefully balance the books. Two, the symbol of the offering is broken when the ushers remove it from the plates at the back of the sanctuary and empty plates are placed on the altar.

The offering is a symbol, but it is an important symbol. Symbols have meaning only when they are regularly interpreted and enacted by those who would know and appreciate the meaning. Obedient sacrifice before God is a theme genuine worship cannot avoid. Every effort possible must be made to incorporate such an emphasis through theologically sound corporate offering.

Worship also involves dedication and commitment. In one sense, this element is not a separate component of worship. Everything from praise to prayer, proclamation to offering involves dedication and commitment when it is done properly. But at the same time, New Testament worship as evidenced on the day of Pentecost offered an opportunity for specific dedication and commitment on the part of the worshipers. Such an opportunity in contemporary worship should never become a means of cheap manipulation of people to "join the church" or to "turn over a new leaf" or to "give their support to the fine pastor and church staff." Specific dedication and commitment, whether the first time or a renewed time, can be uplifting for the congregation who behold the act and seek to support that one with their prayers and undergirding.

It is, indeed, unfortunate that many ministers devote little time to planning the worship event. Not only do a large segment of ministers seem to spend little time or concern in preparing to preach but also an even higher percentage give little or no attention to the remaining two-thirds of the worship hour. Little or no variety is offered in the format of worship. Prayers are done haphazardly and repetitiously. Music is selected at random, following no central theme and providing little freshness. Lay people are viewed basically as passive spectators with little opportunity to be directly involved in worship. The components of worship might be well understood, and yet they will not uplift the worshipers unless there is thoughtful planning involved. The next chapter will offer some ideas of this vital planning.

Notes

1. Robert W. Bailey, *God's Questions and Answers* (New York: Seabury Press, 1977).

2. Donald G. Miller, *The Way to Biblical Preaching* (Nashville: Abingdon Press, 1957), p. 7.

3. Robert W. Bailey, "The Revitalization of the Preaching Event with Emphasis Upon Lay Participation and Perception," An unpublished S.T.D. dissertation, The Southern Baptist Theological Seminary, Louisville, Kentucky, 1970, pp. 3-4.

4. Emil Brunner, *Revelation and Reason* (Philadelphia: The Westminster Press, 1946), p. 142.

5. Robert W. Bailey, "The Revitalization of the Preaching Event," pp. 9 *ff.*

Part II
Planning for Worship

Lack of insight and planning constitutes a real barrier to stimulating and inspiring worship. Just as it is difficult for a preacher to pull together a good sermon week after week when he begins his preparation on Wednesday—or Saturday—it is all but impossible for a cohesive and uplifting design for worship to be conceived and birthed the few days before Sunday. The crucial key is laying out the design for worship weeks, preferably months, in advance. From the themes that are set aside for particular Sundays, fresh and insightful worship can be called forth.

This section is devoted to enabling the reader to design an overview for worship for a year. Then specific guidance is offered in the fifth chapter to aid in planning the worship event for a particular Sunday.

Obviously there is more to worship than planning. There must be intensity and dedication on the part of the worship leaders. There must also be involvement and honesty on the part of the worshipers, including the leaders. However, each of these vital ingredients is more likely to be present when the worship leader has planned an event that will be challenging to him and that will engage the congregation at numerous points.

4
Planning Worship for a Year

At least three essential sources should be considered when plans for the year's worship are laid out. Underlying these sources is a thoughtful awareness of the needs of the people within the church and outside the faith who are participating in the church. Careful prayer and responsiveness to the leading of the Holy Spirit will illumine the reservoir of themes to develop from the Christian Year, the denominational year, and the civil calendar.

While a great many denominations have observed the Christian Year faithfully, numerous churches have been ignorant of or oblivious to the wealth of religious tradition and scriptural inspiration from this resource. The vast importance of the Christian Year to worship necessitates a brief description of the major festivals of the year.

The Christian Year follows the substance of the early apostolic preaching. The themes that have developed and been used for centuries have flowed from the rich heritage of our Christian forebearers. The Christian Year calendar begins four Sundays prior to Christmas. This season of the year is called *Advent*. The theme of these weeks is *preparation*. The coming of Christmas signals the dawning of a new age, the arrival of God's coming on earth in human flesh. The celebration of Christmas can be rather routine, customary, and quickly over, or these weeks can be devoted to the preparation for this singular event of God breaking into human history, thereby heightening the meaning and significance of the celebration of Christmas. Almost every American begins to shop and decorate prior to Christmas Eve or a few days before Christmas. This tradition in the Christian Year allows Christians to achieve more than a passing encounter with the meaning and significance of Christmas.

Christmastide follows Advent. It is the one or two Sundays, depending on what day of the week Christmas comes, that fall between Christmas Day and January 6. The theme of this season is *receiving,* emphasizing our receiving the continued gift of love and life God offers us through his Son, Jesus. Christmas crystalizes the past, present, and future by reminding us what God has done, what God is doing, and what God will do for us by his coming to us and living and working through us. Christmastide lasts twelve days, from Christmas day to the sixth of January.

Epiphany begins on January 6. This season focuses on *man's gift to God.* Epiphany literally means "uncovering," "revealing" or "manifesting" and is tied to the response of the Wise Men to the Christ child. Themes of these weeks include an evangelistic application of the gospel to all of life. Brotherhood Sunday or Race Relations Sunday is part of this period. Jesus' baptism, first miracle in Canaan, as well as the pilgrimage into Egypt, are key concepts in addition to an evangelistic thrust. Into the darkest season of the year and usually the most placid time in the church comes the glorious revealing of God unto all people! This season lasts for four to nine weeks, varying with the dating of Christmas and the dating of Easter.

Lent is for Easter what Advent is for Christmas. This is a forty-day preparation for the celebration of the resurrection of Christ. The themes of this season are *discipline* and *sacrifice.* The use of forty days parallels the recurring theme of forty in the Bible, from the Israelites' forty years in the wilderness to Jesus' forty days in the wilderness. These weeks are crucial for self-examination, self-denial, and heartfelt repentance in order that believers might be able to receive God's great act of love and redemption. Though termed forty days, actually this period counts forty days plus Sundays. The dating of Easter is determined by the first Sunday after the first full moon after the spring equinox, so the timing of Lent varies each year. There are six Sundays in Lent. The fifth Sunday is known as Passion Sunday and the sixth Sunday is commonly known as Palm Sunday.

The Thursday of the week before Easter is known as *Maundy Thursday.* The word *Maundy* comes from the Latin word for "mandate," referring to the new commandment Jesus gave the disciples when they gathered for their last meal prior to his betrayal and crucifixion. Christians for centuries have enjoyed celebrating communion on this special day of the year, remembering both what Christ experienced and what the disciples were doing within themselves on that night.

Friday before Easter is called *Good Friday.* Earlier it was probably known as "God's Friday," the day on which the Son of God was shamefully put to death. Even though sinners nailed Jesus to the cross, the love of the Father in him was not quenched. He suffered like each and every one of us would suffer, yet he offered forgiveness and acceptance for those who would accept it. Worship is, indeed, awesome on this day of the year.

Eastertide is the next season of the Christian Year. Though the Christian Year rightfully begins near the point of Jesus' birth, Easter was the first great Christian event celebrated by the early Christians. The theme of this season is the *proclamation of triumph, joy, hope, victory, and faith.* The wonder of Easter is not concluded with the single day. Just as the disciples felt a spiritual low and serious questioning following the resurrection day, Christians today go through their times of "post-Easter blues." Not only on the Sunday following Easter known as Low Sunday but also on the subsequent weeks of this season, the resounding of the themes indicated will greatly strengthen the Christian life of the congregation.

Pentecost means "fifty" and follows fifty days after the

Passover. Therefore, this season of the Christian Year begins seven Sundays after Easter. The theme is the spectacular awareness of the *birth of the church* and the *presence of the Holy Spirit* for all who will receive Christ as Lord. Of vital importance is an accurate interpretation of the witness of the 120 Christians on the day of Pentecost who did not, according to Acts 2, speak in "unknown" tongues, but who spoke in "other tongues," the languages of the Jewish people who had gathered from around the Mediterranean world to celebrate this high day. The miracle of Pentecost was not some unintelligible gibberish but the fact that the disciples who came from various linguistic backgrounds proclaimed their faith in the resurrected Son of God in their own language other than the Aramaic spoken in Jerusalem. All their fellow countrymen heard and understood—and 3000 became followers that day!

Trinity Sunday is the Sunday following Pentecost. Only after the awareness of the coming of God's Holy Spirit did those first Christians begin to verbalize the one God who had manifested himself in three ways—Father/Creator, Son/Savior, and Spirit/Companion. In order to realize the fuller dimensions of God's self-revelation and not ignore how he relates to man, a careful treatment of the Trinity is vitally important.

Some Christian traditions call the Sundays from Trinity Sunday to Advent the Trinity Season, comprised of twenty-three to twenty-seven weeks, depending on the dating of Easter and what day of the week Christmas falls on. Other Christians have viewed the weeks after Pentecost to the next to the last Sunday of August as *Pentecost Season* and the Sundays from the last Sunday of August to Advent as *Kingdomtide*. In either event, the emphases have been similar. The teachings of Jesus with his insights on ethical and moral problems are the focal point. The later weeks underscore Christ and his kingship and seek to bring the gospel to bear on the full dimensions of life and human relationships.

One additional Sunday of particular significance falls on the

last Sunday of October and is known as *Reformation Sunday.*
This marks the date of Martin Luther's declaration of desired
reforms in the early sixteenth century. The theme is *repentance.*
As it was important for the church to experience repentance instead of penance in 1519, so it continues to remain important
for the church in our day!

A table for the special dates in the Christian Year are printed
on page 49 to help you see the timing and flow of these vital
festivals in the life of Christians both around the world and
across the centuries.

Another advantage of using the Christian Year in planning
worship is that there are a number of good sources of Scripture
readings for each Sunday of the year. Tied in to the themes of
the movement of the Christian faith throughout the year, texts
from the Old Testament and New Testament can provide insight for the particular Sunday. Following through the entire
scheme of the movement of God through Christ can also free a
church from being subjected to the petty whims and narrow
insights of a minister short on ideas. The chart that begins on
page 50 offers a suggested Old Testament and New Testament
reading for each Sunday, beginning with Advent. The number
of Sundays in Epiphany and Trinity Season will vary according
to when Easter comes.

Calendar of the Christian Year

Year	Sundays after Epiphany	First Sunday in Lent	Easter	Pentecost	Trinity	Sundays after Trinity	First Sunday in Advent
1981	8	Mar. 8	Apr. 19	June 7	June 14	23	Nov. 29
1982	7	Feb. 28	Apr. 11	May 30	June 6	24	Nov. 28
1983	6	Feb. 20	Apr. 3	May 22	May 29	25	Nov. 27
1984	9	Mar. 11	Apr. 22	June 10	June 17	23	Dec. 2
1985	6	Feb. 24	Apr. 7	May 26	June 2	25	Dec. 1
1986	5	Feb. 16	Mar. 30	May 18	May 25	26	Nov. 30
1987	8	Mar. 8	Apr. 19	June 7	June 14	23	Nov. 29
1988	6	Feb. 21	Apr. 3	May 22	May 29	25	Nov. 27
1989	5	Feb. 12	Mar. 26	May 14	May 21	27	Dec. 3
1990	8	Mar. 4	Apr. 15	June 3	June 10	24	Dec. 2
1991	5	Feb. 17	Mar. 31	May 19	May 26	26	Dec. 1
1992	8	Mar. 8	Apr. 19	June 7	June 14	23	Nov. 29
1993	7	Feb. 28	Apr. 11	May 30	June 6	24	Nov. 28
1994	6	Feb. 20	Apr. 3	May 22	May 29	25	Nov. 27
1995	5	Mar. 5	Apr. 16	June 4	June 11	24	Dec. 3
1996	6	Feb. 25	Apr. 7	May 26	June 2	25	Dec. 1
1997	5	Feb. 16	Mar. 30	May 18	May 25	26	Nov. 30
1998	7	Mar. 1	Apr. 12	May 31	June 7	24	Nov. 29
1999	6	Feb. 21	Apr. 4	May 23	May 30	25	Nov. 28
2000	9	Mar. 12	Apr. 23	June 11	June 18	23	Dec. 3

Scripture Readings for the Christian Year
November 29, 1981 to November 21, 1982

Sundays & Special Days	*Dates*	*Old Testament*	*New Testament*
ADVENT—Expectancy			
1st Sunday in Advent	11-29-81	Isa. 40:1-11	Rom. 13:8-14
2nd in Advent	12-6	Isa. 35	Luke 1:39-56
3rd in Advent	12-13	Isa. 11:1-16	Luke 3:1-6
4th in Advent	12-20	Isa. 32:1-8	Luke 2:15-20
CHRISTMAS DAY	12-25	Isa. 9:2-7	Luke 2:1-20
1st Sunday after Christmas	12-27	Isa. 45:14-25	John 1:1-14
2nd after Christmas	1-3-82	Josh. 1:1-11	Matt. 2:1-12
EPIPHANY—Evangelistic			
1st Sunday after Epiphany	1-10	Isa. 60	Luke 2:39-52
2nd after Epiphany	1-17	Isa. 41:1-20	John 2:1-11
3rd after Epiphany	1-24	Ruth 1:1-18	1 John 3:1-8
4th after Epiphany	1-31	Prov. 3	Matt. 8:1-13
5th after Epiphany	2-7	Isa. 2:6-22	Eph. 2:11-22
6th after Epiphany	2-14	Jer. 17:5-8	Rom. 3:21-26; 5:18-21
7th after Epiphany	2-21	Isa. 61	Col. 3:12-17
LENT—Renewal			
1st Sunday in Lent	2-28	Isa. 58	Matt. 4:1-11
2nd in Lent	3-7	Dan. 1:8-21	1 Thess. 4:1-12
3rd in Lent	3-14	Mic. 6:6-8	1 John 2:7-17
4th in Lent	3-21	Hos. 14:1-9	Matt. 20:17-28
5th in Lent	3-28	Jer. 26:1-16	John 6:25-35
PALM SUNDAY	4-4	Isa. 52:13 to 53:12	Mark 11:1-10
Maundy Thursday	4-8	Jer. 31:31-34	John 13:1-17
Good Friday—Cross	4-9	Ps. 22	Matt. 27:33-50
Sat. before Easter	4-10	Hos. 6:1-6	1 Peter 3:17-22

EASTER—

Resurrection	4-11	Isa. 25:1-9	John 20:1-10

1st Sunday after

Easter	4-18	Isa. 43:1-13	John 20:19-29
2nd after Easter	4-25	Ezek. 34:11-16	John 21:1-14
3rd after Easter	5-2	1 Sam. 2:1-10	1 Pet. 2:11-25
4th after Easter	5-9	Job 19:21-27a	Rom. 6:1-14
5th after Easter	5-16	Lev. 19:1-18	Jas. 1:17-27
6th after Easter	5-23	Ps. 19	Luke 24:44-53

PENTECOST—

Holy Spirit	5-30	Ezek. 37:1-14	Acts 2:1-11

TRINITY SUNDAY—

Church	6-6	Isa. 6:1-8	2 Cor. 13:14

1st Sunday after

Trinity	6-13	Josh. 24:14-28	Eph. 4:1-16
2nd after Trinity	6-20	Josh. 1	Col. 3:1-17
3rd after Trinity	6-27	2 Sam. 12:1-7a	1 John 3:13-18
4th after Trinity	7-4	Josh. 6:1-20	Acts 2:37-47
5th after Trinity	7-11	1 Kings 17: 17-24	Acts 3:1-10
6th after Trinity	7-18	Deut. 18:9-22	Acts 3:11-26
7th after Trinity	7-25	Ezek. 14	Luke 5:1-11
8th after Trinity	8-1	Jer. 13:1-11	Matt. 5:1-16
9th after Trinity	8-8	Judg. 7:1-23	Matt. 5:17-26
10th after Trinity	8-15	Prov. 2:1-15	Matt. 5:27-37
11th after Trinity	8-22	Ps. 25	Matt. 5:38-48
12th after Trinity	8-29	Ruth 2:1-16	Matt. 6:1-15
13th after Trinity	9-5	1 Sam. 3	Matt. 6:19-34
14th after Trinity	9-12	1 Kings 19:1-8	Matt. 7:1-6
15th after Trinity	9-19	1 Sam. 16:1-13	Matt. 7:7-14
16th after Trinity	9-26	Ps. 116	Matt. 7:15-23
17th after Trinity	10-3	Prov. 10:23-32	Matt. 7:24-29
18th after Trinity	10-10	Mal. 2:4-9	Luke 7:1-10
19th after Trinity	10-17	Mal. 3:13 to 4:5	Eph. 6:10-20

20th after Trinity	10-24	Deut. 4:1-8	Mark 10:17-31
21st after Trinity—Reformation			
Sunday	10-31	Ps. 16	Phil. 1:3-11
22nd after Trinity	11-7	Ps. 1	Phil. 3:17-21
23rd after Trinity	11-14	Ps. 29	Phil. 4:4-9
24th after Trinity	11-21	Jer. 23:1-8	Luke 14:1-11

Regular use of these Scripture readings will enable a church to hear God's Word proclaimed from the Old and New Testaments. It will focus on specific, important themes of the Christian faith and will afford opportunities for series of sermons. One example is the ten-week New Testament reading series from the Sermon on the Mount during Trinity.

Careful attention to such a use of Scripture readings in worship throughout the year will enable congregations to devise their own plan each year or to use similar Scripture passages printed each year.

A second resource for planning worship for a year is the civil calendar. While careful attention should be given to avoiding civil religion, or a practice of Christianity that is wedded to the government and its policies, there is real wisdom in taking into account the attitudes of the congregation during various public celebrations. From New Year's Day to Thanksgiving Day, there are Sundays that lend themselves to a religious interpretation. Memorial Day, July 4, and Labor Day offer possibilities for the worship of the Sunday adjacent to that day being developed around the respective theme. Mother's Day, Children's Day, and Father's Day are usually printed on the civil calendar, and they also provide an important focus in an age when the family is coming unraveled at the seams.

The third resource suggested for planning worship is that of the denominational calendar. Most churches have access to this annual calendar several months in advance. On it are listed such dates as state, national, and worldwide mission emphases. Some denominations focus on Christian citizenship and world hunger. Some have special dates for evangelism, stewardship, Christian education, and various social causes. Some of these dates are constant year after year, while other dates change annually.

The crucial element in planning worship for a year is to have available and be thoroughly familiar with all three calendars described in this chapter. The use of a large planning calendar, preferably one that folds out on one large page, will enable the worship planner to zero in on the various themes to be covered for an entire year. When this work is done thoughtfully and prayerfully, there will not need to be a great deal of rescheduling. The beauty of this type of planning is that music, special worship aids, and preaching can all begin weeks before a particular Sunday. Any time plans are rushed and developed at the last minute, the results will never be as pleasing, careful, and mature as those plans which begin well in advance and have time to incubate, hatch, and develop prior to being used.

Every church needs to experience worship in its fullest possible limits. Worship does not just happen. It takes planning in order to have variety, freshness, enlightenment, and vitality in the worship event Sunday after Sunday. Spiritually led worship can be planned in advance rather than expecting it to happen on Saturday night or come together on Sunday morning. Every congregation will benefit greatly and grow joyfully when they are fed a diet of planned worship experiences which are led and blessed by the Holy Spirit.

5
Planning Worship for a Sunday

At the outset of this crucial planning, the worship leader must have determined a theme for the worship event. Whether that theme comes from the Christian Year calendar, the denominational calendar, the civil calendar, a sermon series, or a local church emphasis—worship which lacks a unity will clearly reveal that fact!

A second vital step to the week's planning is to see the coming experience of worship in light of the three or four weeks preceding it. Better yet, worship will have greater variety and vitality each week when a master plan for worship is laid out ten to twelve weeks at a time. One obvious benefit of this approach is that the congregation will not use the same form to begin the worship weekly. On the other hand, some significant congregational opportunities for involvement will not be overlooked due to the shortsightedness of a single week.

Pre-worship hour plans are vital. The emphasis is placed on *pre*—meaning at least five to ten minutes prior to the stated hour of worship. Normally music is used to help aid the worshipers enter into a spirit of worship. Organ, other instrumental, or choral music might be alternated at this pivotal point for the worship event. A written word may be included in the order of worship that would offer a thought about worship, a prayer to prepare for worship, or a guide for preparing to worship. Variety and promptness are essential keys to this aspect of the worship experience. Also, this is one of two places where discrete announcements could be made without disrupting the flow of worship. The other similar time would come just before the benediction.

Praise should come at the outset of worship. Praise may be offered through music and the spoken word. The congregation is alerted to the theme and purpose for worship through a call to worship. This may be spoken by a worship leader, printed for congregational response, or sung by the choir or the congregation. Occasionally a passage of Scripture can be employed for use at this time, though normally a tailor-made statement about the theme of worship or a general statement or praise is essential. Some examples of various orders of worship will be included in Part IV of this book. Some very practical suggestions for preparing such components of worship are included in Temp Sparkman's book, *Writing Your Own Worship Materials*.[1] All ideas and synonyms on the day's theme need to be jotted down and then a decision made about the form to be used. Finally, a monological or dialogical statement can be devised to capture the meaning of this initial segment of worship.

Hymns are used at several points in the worship event. Care must be taken to assure that the hymns are theologically sound and appropriate for the day's theme. A record of hymns sung should be maintained by the one selecting the hymns in order to avoid singing the same hymn more than once or twice a year and to enable the congregation to sing more of the hymns in the hymnal. Most often a general hymn of praise and adoration is the first hymn sung in the worship hour. Dedicatory and commitment hymns are sung later.

Prayers in worship need to be planned. This does not mean that every prayer is to be written out—indeed, there may be no written prayers. In order to have specific, unified prayers that deal with a particular point in worship, planning and meditation must be given to this assignment in advance.

The invocation is a brief, pointed prayer that invokes God's presence and leadership in the worship experience. This is not a little pastoral prayer. It should never be lengthy. Sometimes it may be a printed unison or a printed responsive prayer. Occasionally the choir or the congregation may sing this prayer. This prayer does not just happen—preparation must be made![2]

The central prayer of the morning or the pastoral prayer needs to be thought out in terms of the theme of the day. Additional concern should be devoted to any critical needs in the church, the community, and/or the world. Sometimes the worship leader may guide the congregation in periods of silent prayer, concluding the prayer time with a brief prayer not more than a paragraph in length.[3] By planning ahead, the choir can be used at times to sing a response to the prayer. The congregation also might sing a conclusion or response to this prayer. The length of the prayer will vary, though it will average between two to five minutes.

The offertory prayer is another time that demands a specific, brief prayer. It may be prayed before the offering is given or after the gifts are presented. The worship leader may pray or the worshipers may pray this prayer. Thoughtful experience will enable both types of offertory prayers to be used.[4] A decision must be made about when the congregation will sing a response to the offering given, using this form every four to eight weeks on an average.

A variety of music can be used during the offertory. Organ, piano, a combination of the two, other instruments or choral music all lend themselves well to this portion of the worship event. An effort to coordinate the music with the worship leader will allow for a diversity at this point.

Choral music frequently is overlooked in the worship planning. The unified worship experience is complete only when the music fits the remainder of the hour. By giving the theme of the day to the music leader two to three months in advance, there is no reason why the music cannot be planned to coordinate with the rest of the day. As with the hymns, a thorough record of anthems sung should be maintained in order to avoid repeating the same piece more than once a year or two or three times every five years. On the other hand, such a record will remind the musicians of an appropriate anthem used in the past that should be sung again a couple of years later.

The Scriptures have theoretically been a central dimension of the worship experience. Without planning for directness of the text and variety in its reading, the Bible reading can become dull and lifeless. Care must be taken to read from the Old Testament and Epistles as well as reading from the Gospels. Frequently more than one passage may be read with meaning and enlightenment. The Scriptures may be done by a worship leader as a unison congregational reading, responsive congregational reading, choral reading by the choir, responsive reading by worship leaders, or a song or anthem in some select instances. In addition to key texts from the Bible, an occasional appropriate reading by a contemporary Christian author will prove illustrative and effective.

Silence is a dimension of worship that must be planned with care. In this age of noise, many people are uncomfortable with silence. Those churches who broadcast over radio or television will have a technical problem at this point, but every congregation needs nurturing in the discipline of silence whereby the worshipers learn to commune with the Father. Prior to the worship hour almost every week and occasionally before or after the pastoral prayer are key times for silence. Another appropriate place for planning silence is following the benediction prior to leaving the church. The congregation seated for a half-minute in silence can solidify the thrust of the worship experience for the coming week.

The *sermon* must be planned and prepared before Saturday night if the power of God's Spirit is to be heard in it. Unfortunately most of the emphasis on preparation has been placed on the sermon, when in fact, planning is crucial for the entire hour. However, care must be taken not to avoid or overlook the demanding discipline of thorough sermonic preparation that results in rightly dividing the word of truth. Such preparation affords the congregation the opportunity of hearing sermons preached from Genesis to Revelation, but never on the same Sunday! Unified themes of the worship event can be clarified and interpreted in the sermon in a life-changing manner. Some have suggested that an hour of preparation is vital for each minute preached.

Commitment does not just happen in worship unless it is anticipated and an opportunity provided for it. A spoken invitation can always follow a sermon prior to the closing hymn. An effective variation is a written call to discipleship in the order of worship following the sermon. Whatever the church's practice may be concerning worshipers sharing a commitment to the Word proclaimed, this portion of the worship must be clear and specific in order to be effective.

The *conclusion* of the worship hour has several important ingredients that must be planned weekly in order to go smoothly. If new members are to be presented to the church, this should be done at this point with preciseness and clarity to facilitate the church becoming acquainted with the new people. If announcements and welcome were not done at the outset of worship, they could be done briefly and tastefully before the benediction. Only the most crucial congregational reminders should be used during the worship hour, for this is not a promotional time for man but an encounter time with God. The printed bulletin is a guide to worship, not promotion.

The benediction may be spoken by the worship leader with a congregational response, a choral response, or a congregational musical response. At times the congregation may do a responsive benediction or a musical benediction. For a change, the choir might do a choral benediction and the minister close the worship experience with a pastoral blessing. A well-rehearsed organ dismissal will prepare the people to return to their lives in the world.

Headings in the order of worship need to be clear and self-explanatory. There are two options for section titles. One is to have a set format with a change only several times a year. The other option is to have the headings be descriptive of the worship event, and thus change each week.[5] The congregation needs to be educated about changes in the order of worship so they will heartily embrace change with reason instead of becoming confused or indifferent to innovative things. The wording and divisions of the worship event can help prepare, motivate, and lead the worshipers in a genuine encounter with God. It will not happen easily, quickly, or automatically, but it can happen.

Worship leaders include the staff but need not be limited to the professional church staff. Men, students, youth, women, and older children all need training by the minister to lead in corporate worship. Lay worship leaders make two points clear. One, worship is not a one-man show involving the minister only. Two, lay persons can lead in worship in the sanctuary, and they can do the same at home! Care should be taken in the selection and training of worship leaders; but by all means, persons other than staff need to be involved in the leadership of worship.

Periodically a group of lay persons might be called together for the purpose of aiding the staff in discussing and designing the worship event. Such an approach can lend freshness and vitality to the planning process and can assure that what is being done is not coming across as abstract concepts to the congregation.

God gives his spiritual leaders minds, and the church gives them time to think and plan. Worship planned carefully each week is no inhibition to the working of the Spirit. Indeed, such planning affords avenues and outlets for the working of the Spirit in the hearts, minds, and lives of those who worship God together. Good, careful planning can result in stimulating, life-changing worship.

Notes

1. G. Temp Sparkman, *Writing Your Own Worship Materials* (Valley Forge: Judson Press, 1980).
2. Ibid., pp. 27-33.
3. Ibid., pp. 55-59.
4. Ibid., pp. 97-104.
5. Ibid.

Part III
Tools for Evaluating Worship

Worship is frequently done mindlessly. Approaches and forms are repeated aimlessly from one church to another, from one decade to another, and from one context to another. Some aspects of worship may be theologically unsound or biblically inaccurate. One congregation may be stimulated to worship in a fashion that would be most uninspiring to another group of believers. In order to ascertain the authenticity of the worship experience and how accurately it speaks to the needs and expectations of the congregation, worship must be periodically evaluated. This portion of the book is devoted to describing some viable tools of evaluation and to offering some sample forms for this purpose.

6
Approaches for Evaluation

Two primary questions should be raised when evaluating worship. One, is it theologically sound? Two, is it engaging the people in a genuine encounter with God? Several evaluation approaches are available to obtain answers to these questions.

Initially the minister and other staff members need to reflect honestly on the design and content of the worship hour. Several concerns need to be resolved by this level of leadership. Ongoing, searching evaluation of worship by the staff is vitally important to developing a growing encounter with God by the church.

Another approach is to select or elect a group of lay persons to assist in worship evaluation. These representative, interested church members can become involved in evaluating the present worship. They might also be used to help devise new forms of worship. This group could meet regularly or periodically, depending on whether they are providing continued or occasional input to the worship process. Dialogue with such a body can help eliminate the gray, fuzzy areas in worship and facilitate theologically sound worship that will stimulate personal involvement among the people.

A third possibility is to invite the entire congregation to evaluate worship through written questionnaires. Brief evaluation forms could be completed at the conclusion of morning worship. Longer questionnaires necessitate an abbreviated worship experience in order to provide the fifteen to twenty minutes needed to complete the forms. A smaller percentage of return could be obtained by mailing out the questionnaires to all members and having them return them on Sunday or through the mail. Sample evaluations appear in the next chapter.

Worship dialogue is another approach for evaluation. Following a luncheon at the church after morning worship or on Sunday or Wednesday evening, a discussion period can be scheduled for the congregation to express itself on the form and content of worship in its church. The minister and any other staff members must be comfortable enough with their work that they can encounter objections without becoming defensive and objectionable themselves. While some may use such a time for personal complaints, most will view it as an opportunity for honest reflection.

The dialogue should begin with the minister or worship committee member restating the intent of worship that Sunday or in that church in general. The members should be encouraged to be honest and objective without mixing personalities into their discussion of their view of worship. A facilitator for the open discussion is essential —one who can ask good leading questions and one who can direct the discussion on the subject at hand. Such a dialogue might be held once a year or could well be a several-week series periodically.

The staff needs to be prepared to deal with any and all suggestions—not necessarily on the spot, but in the following weeks. The biblically unsound ideas can be dealt with through preaching and teaching on Christian worship. The positive ideas should be incorporated in the worship experience at the earliest opportunity.

Evaluation can open the way for improved worship. The twofold key is obtaining the proper tools for evaluation and then making wise use of the findings of the evaluation.

7
Sample Evaluations

The body of this chapter is devoted to ideas for evaluations that might be used in your church. If you desire to use an evaluation verbatim, request copyright permission and give proper credit on your form. Identification of the questionnaire is provided at the top for your assistance.

For the Staff

Check one for each question: *Yes   No   Uncertain*

1. Is the main effort of the worship we lead to entertain the congregation?
2. Do the worship leaders view themselves as the sole performers?
3. Are the lay people involved in planning the worship experience?
4. Are the lay people involved in leading the worship event?
5. Are the worshipers directed in a specific encounter with God?
6. Is the Bible reading and interpretation central in worship?
7. Is there variety in the format of worship?
8. Do the hymns and anthem provide accurate biblical interpretation?
9. Are the worshipers allowed to

participate in worship other than
by singing or listening?
10. Is there significant variety and
change in the various elements of
worship?
11. How much time is spent weekly in
designing the worship event?   ½-1 hr. 1-3 hr. 4-8 hr.
12. How important is worship to the
church?   Very   moderate   little

For the Church

1. Brief questionnaire inserted in order of worship, to leave at
door.
   (1) I found the worship experience today to be (check one:)
   ___ "a joyful, meaningful, uplifting and/or helpful experience;
   ___ a dull, lifeless and comparatively uninspiring experience;
   ___ somewhere in between those two."[1]
   (2) Today I felt the sermon (check one:)
   ___ "spoke directly to the concerns and questions I
   brought with me;
   ___ was interesting, but not especially relevant to me;
   ___ was neither interesting nor very helpful."[2]
   (3) The most stimulating and helpful aspect of the worship
   experience for me today was (check one only:)
   ___ anthems/special music
   ___ prayers
   ___ congregational singing
   ___ congregational readings
   ___ silence
   ___ simply having the opportunity for corporate worship of God
   ___ feeling a part of this unique worshiping Christian
   community

___ opportunity for confession to and forgiveness from
God
___ the varied order of worship
___ the use of lay worship leaders

2. Brief evaluation inserted in order of worship, left at door.

Opinion Survey [3]

I have found the following worship innovations to be:

1. Maundy Thursday Lord's Supper Service	___very helpful	___somewhat helpful	___not helpful	___did not attend
2. The Cross in Baptistry, Easter	___very helpful	___somewhat helpful	___not helpful	
3. Advent Wreath	___very helpful	___somewhat helpful	___not helpful	
4. Moment of Silence, end of service	___very helpful	___somewhat helpful	___not helpful	
5. As a radio listener, have you found the message to shut-ins	___very helpful	___somewhat helpful	___not helpful	___not heard
6. Good Neighbor Night, pulpit guest	___very helpful	___somewhat helpful	___not helpful	
7. Children's Story	___very helpful	___somewhat helpful	___not helpful	
8. Would you find continuing involvement of Laypersons as worship leaders	___very helpful	___somewhat helpful	___not helpful	
9. Pastor wearing robe on Special Services	___very helpful	___somewhat helpful	___not helpful	
10. Dramatic Monologue Sermon	___very helpful	___somewhat helpful	___not helpful	___haven't heard one
11. Congregational use of the Lord's Prayer	___very helpful	___somewhat helpful	___not helpful	

Please check your age group: ___ 12 or under ___ 13-20 ___
21-30 ___ 31-50 ___ above 50 ___
Your suggestions or comments: _____
_____
Thank you for helping make our worship more meaningful.

3. More extensive worship evaluation, to be left at the door. This one is also inserted in the order of worship.[4]

Worship Evaluation

The purpose of this evaluation form is to discover ways to improve the church worship service. After observing a service, answer the questions below based on that one service.

The figures opposite each question indicate varying degrees of effectiveness: 0 for very poor, 1 for poor, 2 for fair, 3 for good, 4 for very good, and 5 for excellent. Circle the figure which, in your opinion, describes the answer in each instance. After each rating, list the factors which determined your choice. To secure a percentage of effectiveness on the basis of your rating, add the figures.

1. Was the meeting place conducive to worship?   0 1 2 3 4 5

2. Did the ushers contribute to the worshipfulness of the service?   0 1 2 3 4 5

3. Were the worship leaders prepared to lead when the service started?   0 1 2 3 4 5

4. Was an appropriate selection and arrangement of worship materials used in the service?   0 1 2 3 4 5

5. Were the hymns appropriate?   0 1 2 3 4 5

6. Was the congregational singing participated in meaningfully?   0 1 2 3 4 5

7. Did the musicians, choir members, and leader refrain from that which would distract the worshipers?   0 1 2 3 4 5

8. Did the musical instruments contribute meaningfully to your worship experience?   0 1 2 3 4 5

9. Were the public prayers helpful to you?   0 1 2 3 4 5

10. Was the Bible handled appropri-
    ately? Was the Scripture passage
    read effectively?   0 1 2 3 4 5
11. Did the offertory present an oppor-
    tunity for worshipful expression?   0 1 2 3 4 5
12. Did the "special" music contribute
    effectively to meaningful worship?   0 1 2 3 4 5
13. Did God seem real to you?   0 1 2 3 4 5
14. Did you worship quietly and rever-
    ently without distraction?   0 1 2 3 4 5
15. Was there evidence of a sense of pur-
    pose and direction in the worship?   0 1 2 3 4 5
16. Did you feel interested in the ser-
    mon?   0 1 2 3 4 5
17. Did the sermon give you new infor-
    mation?   0 1 2 3 4 5
18. Did the sermon inspire you to
    action?   0 1 2 3 4 5
19. Did the invitation seem appropriate
    and effective?   0 1 2 3 4 5
20. Did you respond to the invitation in
    any way?   0 1 2 3 4 5

Possible rating, 100   My rating _____

What was your overall response to the worship experience?_____

_____

What impressed you most favorably?_____

_____

What improvements would you suggest?_____

_____

_____

_____

_____

4. Detailed evaluation, requiring 15-20 minutes with brief sermon or plan to have the questionnaires completed at home
and brought or mailed to the church.[5]

Your Evaluation of Worship in Our Church

Your church leaders feel that worship is a significant function
in which every Christian should be involved. What takes place
on Sunday is not a performance of those on the platform but an
involvement of all persons present under the direction of the
worship leaders.

In order to help the worship leaders know of your insights
and your needs, we request that you complete the following
form. Please answer every question and write in additional
comments if you desire. Please answer exactly as you feel. Your
name is not requested.

I. Background Information
   Would you first give some information about yourself
   by drawing a circle around the answer that applies to
   you?
   1. Age: Under 20   20-29   30-39   40-49   50-59   60-69
          70 or older
   2. Sex: Male   Female
   3. How long ago did you first become a member of any
      church?
      Less than 2 years   2-5 years   6-10 years   11-20 years
      More than 20 years
   4. How long have you been a member of First Baptist
      Church?
      Less than 2 years   2-5 years   6-10 years   11-20 years
      More than 20 years
   5. Marital Status: Married Single Widowed Divorced
   6. Occupation: _____

7. Education (Circle highest grade completed):
1 2 3 4 5 6 7 8 9 10 11 12 College 1 2 3 4
Postgraduate   1   2   3   or more

8. How often have you attended church worship experiences in the last three months?
Every time   Once a week   2 or 3 times a month
Once a month   Less than once a month

II. Evaluation of the Total Worship Event
Which parts of the worship experience are most meaningful to you? Recognizing that all parts of the hour may be significant, try to select which parts are most meaningful to you.

1. Place a 1 in front of the most meaningful part of the worship event.
2. Place a 2 in front of the next most meaningful part of the experience.
3. Place a check mark (✓) in front of the least meaningful part.

____ Congregational singing
____ Scripture
____ Special music
____ Message
____ Organ music
____ Lord's Supper
____ Baptism
____ Prayers
____ Calls to worship, prayer
____ Children's sermons

III. Music in Worship
A. Organ music
Check the blank that indicates your response.
1. Do you find yourself aspiring to and preparing for worship during the prelude?
Very often____ Often____ Occasionally____
Seldom____ Never____
2. Does the offertory provide additional stimulus for your worship?
Very Often____ Often____ Occasionally____
Seldom____ Never____

3. Do you normally listen to the postlude?
   Very Often___ Often___ Occasionally___
   Seldom___ Never___
4. Do you enjoy having special organ accompaniment on the final verse of hymns?
   Very Often___ Often___ Occasionally___
   Seldom___ Never___
5. Do you benefit by having the printed text of organ selections?
   Very Often___ Often___ Occasionally___
   Seldom___ Never___

B. Congregational singing
1. Please list your three favorite hymns.

   _____
   _____
   _____

2. Are you willing to learn to sing new hymns?
   Very Often___ Often. _ Occasionally___
   Seldom___ Never___
3. Would you like a regular opportunity for suggesting hymns to be used?
   Very Often___ Often___ Occasionally___
   Seldom___ Never___

C. Anthems
1. Do you normally enjoy the anthems the choir sings?
   Very Often___ Often___ Occasionally___
   Seldom___ Never___
2. Do you benefit by having the printed text of the choral music presented by the choirs?
   Very Often___ Often___ Occasionally___
   Seldom___ Never___
3. Do you prefer to have the younger choirs to sing more often?

Very Often___ Often___ Occasionally___
Seldom___ Never___
D. Handbells
  1. Do you normally enjoy the handbell music?
     Very Often___ Often___ Occasionally___
     Seldom___ Never___
  2. Would you like the text of the music printed?
     Very Often___ Often___ Occasionally___
     Seldom___ Never___
  3. How frequently would you prefer handbell music?
     Every worship service___ Once a week___
     Twice a month___ Once a month___
     Less than once a month___
  4. Do you prefer a handbell offertory instead of a handbell prelude?
     Very Often___ Often___ Occasionally___
     Seldom___ Never___
E. Other instruments
  1. Do you enjoy the use of other instruments in the worship music?
     Very Often___ Often___ Occasionally___
     Seldom___ Never___
  2. If yes, what instruments do you most enjoy hearing?
     _____

F. Other worship aids
  1. Do you prefer the use of the following choral worship aids?
     a. Choral call to worship
        Very Often___ Often___ Occasionally___
        Seldom___ Never___
     b. Offertory prayer response
        Very Often___ Often___ Occasionally___
        Seldom___ Never___

    c. Benediction response
       Very Often___ Often___ Occasionally___
       Seldom___ Never___
  2. Do you prefer the use of the following music worship aids?
    a. Doxology
       Very Often___ Often___ Occasionally___
       Seldom___ Never___
    b. Glory Be to the Father
       Very Often___ Often___ Occasionally___
       Seldom___ Never___
    c. Offertory Responses
       Very Often___ Often___ Occasionally___
       Seldom___ Never___
    d. How often do you prefer one of the above be used?
       Once a week___ Twice a month___
       Once a month___ Less than once a month___

IV. Scripture
  1. Do you follow the Scripture reading in your Bible?
    Very Often___ Often___ Occasionally___
    Seldom___ Never___
  2. Do you enjoy hearing the Scripture read from different translations?
    Very Often___ Often___ Occasionally___
    Seldom___ Never___
  3. Do you like having an *Old* Testament and a *New* Testament reading?
    Very Often___ Often___ Occasionally___
    Seldom___ Never___
  4. Do you like to hear choral Scripture readings?
    Very Often___ Often___ Occasionally___
    Seldom___ Never___
    How often?

Once a month____   Several times a year____
Once a year____
5. Do you like responsive readings of the Bible?
   Very Often____   Often____   Occasionally____
   Seldom____   Never____
   How frequently?
   Once a month____   Twice a month____
   Three times a month____   Every Sunday____
   More than one reading a Sunday____
6. Do you find meaning in responsive Scripture read-
   ings between worship leaders?
   Very Often____   Often____   Occasionally____
   Seldom____   Never____
   How often?
   Once a year____   Several times a year____
   Once a month____   More often than once a month____
7. Do you enjoy unison Scripture readings?
   Very Often____   Often____   Occasionally____
   Seldom____   Never____
   How frequently?
   Once a week____   Twice a month____
   Once a month____   Less often than once a month____

V. Readings
   1. Do you like a responsive call to worship?
      Very Often____   Often____   Occasionally____
      Seldom____   Never____
   2. Do you find meaning in a corporate confession or
      call to prayer?
      Very Often____   Often____   Occasionally____
      Seldom____   Never____
   3. Do you like a responsive offertory dedication?
      Very Often____   Often____   Occasionally____
      Seldom____   Never____
   4. Do you enjoy praying a responsive invocation?

Very Often____   Often____   Occasionally____
Seldom____   Never____

5. Do you find meaning in a responsive benediction?
Very Often____   Often____   Occasionally____
Seldom____   Never____

6. If you like responses, how often would you like one used?
Once a month____   Twice a month____
Once a week____   More than once a week____
Less than once a month____

VI. Prayers
1. Do you find meaning in praying the Lord's Prayer in unison?
Very Often____   Often____   Occasionally____
Seldom____   Never____

2. Do you prefer silent meditation before the morning prayer?
Very Often____   Often____   Occasionally____
Seldom____   Never____

3. Do you find inspiration for your own prayer during the morning prayer?
Very Often____   Often____   Occasionally____
Seldom____   Never____

4. Do you enjoy singing a prayer, such as "The Lord's Prayer" for the invocation?
Very Often____   Often____   Occasionally____
Seldom____   Never____

VII. Lay Worship Leaders
1. Do you enjoy having lay persons assist in leading the worship service?
Very Often____   Often____   Occasionally____
Seldom____   Never____
How often?

Once a month____   Twice a month____
Three times____   Every week____
Less than once a month____

2. Rank from 1 to 5 in the order of your preference the following categories of worship leaders:
   ____ youth
   ____ college students
   ____ women
   ____ children
   ____ men

3. Is there any category of leader who has failed to lead you effectively in worship?
   Yes____   No____   Undecided____
   If yes, which?_____

VIII. Ordinances

1. Can you see the baptismal service?
   Yes____   No____

2. Can you hear the baptismal service?
   Yes____   No____

3. Do you like the use of the pitcher, cup, and loaf to dramatize the first Lord's Supper?
   Very Often____   Often____   Occasionally____
   Seldom____   Never____

4. Can you hear the minister during the Lord's Supper serving?
   Very Often____   Often____   Occasionally____
   Seldom____   Never____

5. Throughout the year during the celebration of the Lord's Supper,
   a. Do you find meaning in a candlelight service?
      Very Often____   Often____   Occasionally____
      Seldom____   Never____
   b. Do you find meaning in a Sunday morning observance?

Very Often___   Often___   Occasionally___
Seldom___   Never___

   c. Do you find meaning in the dramatic portrayal of the Lord's Supper the Thursday night before Easter?
Yes___   No___   Undecided___
Have not attended___
Prefer not to have the drama included___

6. Do you find meaning in celebrating baptism and the Lord's Supper in the same service?
Very Often___   Often___   Occasionally___
Seldom___   Never___

7. Do you like organ music while you are being served the Lord's Supper?
Very Often___   Often___   Occasionally___
Seldom___   Never___

8. Do you like a silent Lord's Supper service?
Very Often___   Often___   Occasionally___
Seldom___   Never___

IX. Sermon

1. Do you think a sufficient variety of topics is dealt with?
Yes___   No___   Undecided___

2. Do you feel that the length of the sermon is appropriate?
Yes___   No___   Undecided___

3. Do you feel the explanation of the biblical text is adequate and enlightening?
Very Often___   Often___   Occasionally___
Seldom___   Never___

4. Is there a favorite sermon you have heard in the last two years you would like to have repeated?
   a. Yes___   No___

b. If yes, what was the title or the topic?_____

5. Do you like a series of messages?
Yes___ No___ Undecided___

6. Is there a text, topic, or sermon series you would like to hear preached?
a. Yes___ No___ Undecided___
b. If yes, please indicate. _____

7. Would you like regular opportunities for talk-back and discussion of the sermon?
a. Yes___ No___ Undecided___
b. If yes, please check when:
___ After the worship service on Sunday morning
___ Sunday evening during Church Training
___ Wednesday evening (instead of Bible study)

8. Below are several areas involved in presenting the sermon. Check any that you feel needs to be improved by the minister.
Eye contact___ Rapidity of speech___
Gestures___ Variation in tone of voice___
Volume of speech___ Use of notes___
Grammar___ Movement of hands or feet___

9. Do you like the children's sermon?
a. Yes___ No___ Undecided___
b. How long do you feel it should be?
Less than 3 minutes___ About 3 minutes___
More than 3 minutes___
c. How often would you prefer the children's sermon?
Weekly___ Twice a month___
Once in 3 weeks___ Once a month___
d. Would you prefer the children to sit at the front of the sanctuary during the children's sermon?
Yes___ No___ Undecided___

10. Have you found meaning in the varied forms of proclamation used such as drama, films, slides, dramatic musicals, and dramatic readings?
Very Often____ Often____ Occasionally____
Seldom____ Never____
Rank from 1 to 5 your order of preference:
____ drama
____ slides
____ dramatic musicals
____ films
____ dramatic readings

X. Participation in Worship
  1. Theoretically, you are expected to participate in the worship at several points. Do you feel a sense of participation? Circle one response.
     a. In the organ music?
        Very little   Little   Some   Much   Very much
     b. In the hymns?
        Very little   Little   Some   Much   Very much
     c. In the prayers?
        Very little   Little   Some   Much   Very much
     d. In the choral music?
        Very little   Little   Some   Much   Very much
     e. In the Scripture reading?
        Very little   Little   Some   Much   Very much
     f. In the message?
        Very little   Little   Some   Much   Very much
     g. In the children's sermon?
        Very little   Little   Some   Much   Very much
  2. "When you come to church, you should forget for a time the problems and responsibilities you have to deal with all week." Would you agree with this statement?

Strongly agree   Agree   Undecided   Disagree
Strongly disagree
3. How much of a direct connection or relationship do
   you see between what you do during the week and
   what you hear and do during church on Sunday?
   Very little   Little   Some   Much   Very much
4. In the responsibilities, problems, or decisions which
   you face in your work (or home or social life), do
   you ask yourself what the religious perspective or
   Christian answer is for that particular situation?
   Very Often___   Often___   Occasionally___
   Seldom___   Never___

XI. Welcome and Announcements
   1. Do you prefer that the worshipers be welcomed and
      visitors recognized?
      Yes___   No___   Undecided___
   2. Can you hear the names of the new members
      presented and the announcements made?
      Yes___   No___   Most of the time___   Seldom___
   3. Do you think the close of the worship period is the
      best time for important announcements?
      Yes___   No___   Undecided___
      If no, when would you prefer that this be done?___

XII. Sound System
   1. Are you able to easily hear those who speak from the
      pulpit? Circle one response.
      Always   Often   Sometimes   Seldom   Never
   2. If you are unable to hear most speakers,
      a. Which speakers can you not hear?
         Minister   Minister of Education   Lay Leader
      b. Do you wear a hearing aid?
         Yes___   No___

    c. Would you use a hand-held hearing set if it were installed where you sit?
Yes___ No___ Undecided___.

    d. Would you move to designated seats in the sanctuary if hearing sets were installed there?
Yes___ No___ Undecided___

    e. Where do you usually sit?
Left___ Middle___ Right___
Under left balcony___ Under middle balcony___
Under right balcony___ Left balcony___
Right balcony___ Middle balcony___

XIII. Please use this space and the back of this page to indicate any other suggestions or questions on our worship. Please leave this survey in the box at the door.

Notes

1. Lyle E. Schaller, "Evaluating Worship," *The Christian Ministry*, Vol. XI, No. 2, March, 1980, p. 37.

2. Ibid., p. 37.

3. Alton H. McEachern in "Evaluating and Improving Congregational Worship," Robert W. Bailey, *Ideas for Effective Worship Services*, James C. Barry and Jack Gulledge, ed. and compilers (Nashville: Convention Press, 1977), pp. 77-78.

4. John Ishee in "Evaluating and Improving Congregational Worship," p. 79.

5. Robert W. Bailey, "Evaluating and Improving Congregational Worship," pp. 69-75.

Part IV
Worship on Special Days

Every Sunday is a special day! It is a unique opportunity to encounter God in a life-changing experience through corporate worship. If worship is to have fresh meaning each week, continued attempts must be made to interject variety on the one hand and a cohesive theme on the other. Otherwise, worship will neither comfort nor confront, and the hour spent in the sanctuary will not give the worshipers anything to remember, feel, or do.

A close viewing of the ecclesiastical, denominational, civil and local church calendars will reveal a potential emphasis for nearly every Sunday--and indeed, several possible themes for some Sundays! In order to provide some ideas and insights into designing worship for any Sunday, this section of the book will offer annotated illustrations of over twenty Sundays of the year.

Advent

Many churches have been poverty stricken by failing to observe the four weeks prior to Christmas as a time of preparation for celebrating Christ's coming anew into the hearts of all believers. Advent, the beginning of the Christian Year, is the season of preparation and anticipation.

Worship on this day features two special forms of congregational involvement through the responsive opening sentences and the New Testament reading which includes the leader, the choir, and the congregation. The opening sentences are adapted from Frank M. Whitman in *Ventures in Worship, Vol. III,* edited by David James Randolph. Copyright © by Abingdon Press, pp. 31-32. Used by permission.

In this section normally just the order of worship and explanation will be given for each Sunday. However, on this Sunday the sermon is included as a further illustration of how the unified theme is developed throughout the worship event.

Advent is a season of readiness, and that is the purpose of this experience of worship.

THE WORSHIP OF GOD
Third Sunday of Advent

COME, LORD JESUS

SACRED MUSIC
CHORAL CALL TO WORSHIP

OPENING SENTENCES

Leader: We have been instructed to search diligently for the Child.

People: Our trouble is we have desired to find just the *Child!*

Leader: Or we have merely sought to maintain the level of understanding and commitment we had when we were children.

People: It is exciting to move in a new direction, in response to God's guidance,

Leader: And to rejoice with exceeding great joy when we discover the place.

People: What place is that?

Leader: The place where we can experience fully the birth of Christ in our lives.

People: And then we can worship.

Leader: This can be the place! We can bring the full gifts of our lives to God in joyful thanksgiving for what he has done for us through his Son, Jesus!

People: Hallelujah! Amen!

INVOCATION

HYMN   "Angels We Have Heard on High"   arr. by Angell

GREETING THE WORSHIPERS

DUET

THOU SON OF GOD

THE OLD TESTAMENT READING   Jeremiah 31:15-22

THE NEW TESTAMENT READING   Matthew 2:13-18

Leader: Now when they had departed, behold, an angel of the Lord appeared to Joseph in a dream and said,

Choir: "Rise, take the child and his mother, and flee to Egypt, and remain there till I tell you; for Herod is about to search for the child, to destroy him."

People: And he rose and took the child and his mother by night, and departed to Egypt, and remained there until the death of Herod. This was to fulfil

	what the Lord had spoken by the prophet,
Choir:	"Out of Egypt have I called my son."
Leader:	Then Herod, when he saw that he had been tricked by the wise men, was in a furious rage, and he sent and killed all the male children in Bethlehem and in all that region who were two years old or under, according to the time which he had ascertained from the wise men.
People:	Then was fulfilled what was spoken by the prophet Jeremiah:
Choir:	"A voice was heard in Ramah, wailing and loud lamentation, Rachel weeping for her children; she refused to be consoled, because they were no more."

MUSICAL MEDITATION
MORNING PRAYER

THOU SON OF MAN

HYMN   "It Came upon the Midnight Clear"   Willis
MORNING OFFERING
    Offertory Prayer
    Instrumental Offertory

BE KNOWN TO US TODAY

ANTHEM
MESSAGE   "Weeping for the Children"
HYMN   "Thou Didst Leave Thy Throne"   Matthews
PRESENTATION OF NEW MEMBERS
BENEDICTION
INSTRUMENTAL DISMISSAL

Weeping for the Children

Matthew 2:13-18
Jeremiah 31:15-22

I can still remember that cold December day as though it were yesterday, when in fact it was 1968. My wife and I drove with her parents to Atlanta to bid farewell to her brother. He was a Lieutenant in the Marines who was being sent to Vietnam. What an anxiety-filled day it was! We tried to talk, but no conversation would last long. We tried to laugh, but humor had long since dried up within us. We tried to hope, but twelve months on the other side of the world in the midst of a great struggle against Communism seemed so overwhelming.

I recall my father-in-law looking at his only son. I am sure that man was remembering World War II in which he fought and was injured. I know he must have been thinking about all the things he and his son had done together and wanted yet to do together. Now this war was pulling them apart with the threat of never being together again.

I remember my mother-in-law looking at her youngest child. Since that time I have become a parent, and I sense the agony she felt as she watched that young man, who had been an infant in her arms, walk away for the plane. He had been away from home for several years while in college and serving in the Marines in the States, but it seemed this single event of his leaving would literally break her heart.

I recall my wife and my sister-in-law as they watched the man who was their brother and husband disappear into that plane. I saw my wife who, only thirteen months older than her brother, seemed to be giving up a part of herself. I saw my sister-in-law of two years look with agonizing wonder, not knowing if she would ever see her husband again.

Yes, though many years have passed, I still remember witnessing the trauma of that winter day at the airport when parents were weeping for their child and when all of us wept as he was taken captive by a harsh war. We yearned to reach out to that plane and hold it back so that he would not be swallowed up by the hatred and selfishness that threatened his very existence. In spite of our tears and fears, he went away.

As I recall that experience etched so vividly into my life, I think about the parents today who are weeping for their children who are going into captivity. I think of the parents who see their children run away from home with the idea of finding a better and easier life. I think about the parents who weep for the children who, though they live at home, are far away from them emotionally. I think about the parents who weep for their children who are captive to the gods of materialism—very much like their parents themselves—seeking to keep up with or exceed the things their friends have and the brand names they possess. I think of the parents who weep for their children who are captivated by their peers. At times for apparently no real reason, children turn against their parents just because their friends are down on adults and urge them to turn their backs on their own parents.

I think of parents who weep for children held captive by the forces of evil today—from those who are deceitful and dishonest to those who are on drugs; from those children who steal and slander to those who are absorbed by alcohol; from those children who use their sexuality illicitly to those who refuse to do their best work. I think about parents who weep for children held captive by the evil forces that tempt them to be disrespectful to God, living as though he does not exist—or if he does, does not make any difference to their lives. I think about parents weeping for their children . . . and I weep with them!

Tevye, the central character in the powerful play, *Fiddler on the Roof,* found himself weeping for his children who got caught up in the changing times and abandoned the traditions of his past. His daughters pulled away from the Russian Jewish practice of entering into marriages arranged by the parents through a matchmaker. In his sad, frustrated way, Tevye asked:

> "What's happening to the tradition?
> One little time I pulled out a thread
> And where has it led? Where has it led?"[1]

Parents weep for their children who pull away from them and who do things that hurt themselves. God also weeps for his children who sin and pull away from him. He weeps for the children who never grow up but just keep on living and acting like children all their lives. God weeps for his children who are so insecure they seek to undermine or even destroy those who seem to have the potential of greatness, just as King Herod did. You and I both know people who are vicious in their attacks on others, not because their bitterness is justified but because they want to tear down those whose work and energy elevates them above those vicious persons. God also weeps for his children who suffer because of their own sin and who suffer because of the sins of others.

Herod's brutal destruction of all boy babies under two years of age caused a reign of terror and dismay among the people of Judah. Matthew remembered another time in earlier Jewish history when terror and anxiety had been at a peak. The Israelites were being carried into captivity and on their way into captivity they passed by Ramah, the place where Jacob's wife, Rachel, was buried. The prophet Jeremiah expressed the sadness of this time by saying figuratively that Rachel, the mother of Joseph and Benjamin, wept over the fact that the Israelites were being carried away captive, most of whom would never return to their homeland again. Matthew saw this ugly destruction of life as another time of grave weeping for the children of God.

Sometimes we hurt because of what we do. Other times we hurt because of what others do to us. But in it all man's inhumanity to man is overwhelming. At the end of the 1970s, 120 international wars had been waged during the third of a century since the conclusion of World War II. Most of these wars have been fought in the developing Third-World nations. In these wars brought about because of the greed and hatred of man against man, more than 25 million people have died! How God weeps over the sins of his children!

God weeps for the pain of his children. He weeps over the plight of all hurting people in the world, but most especially those who are little children. I read about a minister who heard a baby's cry in the nativity scene in front of the church. Upon investigation he found a two-day-old baby in the manger along with a note which read: "I'm Timothy—please take care of me." And so this little boy, named by the church community, Timothy Christmas, was abandoned by a mother who did not want him or could not manage to care for him. How God does weep for his children!

Around the world at this very moment, well over a half billion people are starving to death! Some of them live in the United States. Most of them live in war-torn, underdeveloped nations which presently do not have the means or know-how to provide their own food. Cambodia is a classic contemporary example of this plight of the evil complexities of war and lack of food. Most Americans grow fat and anxiously try to lose weight while about one out of four people in the world will die before reaching adulthood simply because they do not have enough adequate food to eat! We spend great time, effort, and money to prepare all our expensive holiday foods while people with no money and no food die! Can we not understand how God weeps for his children—both those who starve and we who fail to have the compassion to help feed them?

A presidential commission reported that unless the United States revises its international policies and helps nations learn to feed themselves, before the end of the century we will have a global hunger crisis that will make the current energy crisis seem mild. Our nation has grown rich in the last thirty years, and in the process we have reduced the amount of nonmilitary aid to weak nations from 12 percent of our gross national product to about 1 percent, all the while we are building bigger and better bombs and arming the world to self-destruct![2] Can you not understand why God is weeping for his children?

In December 1979, a nun in India, who has devoted her life to helping the poor and hungry, received the Nobel Peace Prize for her efforts. Sister Teresa, a small 69-year-old woman, accepted the prize "in the name of the hungry, of the naked, of the homeless, of the blind, of the lepers, of all those who feel unwanted, unloved, uncared for throughout society."³ She announced her plans to use the $192,000 prize money for the poor that their dignity might be restored and their lives lengthened. She asked that the traditional awards banquet be canceled and that money donated to the poor also. Her request was granted and an additional $7,000 was made available by saving the banquet cost!

She believes that the poor need not our sympathy and pity, but our love and understanding. They, too, have been created by God both to love and to be loved. Once when Sister Teresa came to the United States to speak, her host met her plane. Upon seeing the little nun with a small bag in her hand, the host asked about her luggage. She replied as she looked down at her handbag, "This is all I have." Most of us are so busy accumulating more and more things—bigger and better houses, more extravagant and fattening goods—we do not acknowledge that the poor and hungry, the homeless and unwanted even exist! How God weeps for his children—the poor who are starving and those of us who refuse to share our food!

God weeps for the loneliness of his children. Christmas is an exciting time for families, but it is a very lonely and depressing time for the almost 50 million single adults in America. The human potential movement of this decade has revealed how deep the wound of loneliness is in the fabric of American life. A report in the journal of the American Medical Association disclosed that depression is the third most common malady in America today. And valium is the most widely prescribed drug in our nation. Loneliness is the sign of our times when people are so busy worshiping at the shrine of selfish they fail to follow God's directive to care about and be involved in the lives of others.

Even the churches of Jesus Christ are focusing more on body-building programs and achieving self-fulfillment to the exclusion of being concerned with critical world needs. Southern Baptists had a statistic in 1979 that glaringly documents this tendency in the modern church. During the previous eleven years, some 35 thousand Southern Baptist Churches have spent more money paying the *interest* on their new buildings than they did for *all mission causes combined!* That is correct! Southern Baptists spent more money paying the interest on their finer buildings for themselves than they did on all mission causes! Can you fail to realize how God weeps for his children?

God also weeps because of the way his children reject him. God, who came into the world in his unique Son, Jesus Christ, found that mankind still rejected him, hated him, despised him, persecuted him, hurt him, and sought to destroy him. At the end of his ministry, Matthew noted Jesus' summary statement about the rejection of the people: "O Jerusalem, Jerusalem, killing the prophets and stoning those who are sent to you! How often would I have gathered your children together as a hen gathers her brood under her wings, and you would not!" (23:37, RSV) How God weeps over his children who reject him yet today!

All need not be sadness and weeping. God's coming to earth in human flesh can turn weeping into joy, sorrow into purpose, and sadness into meaning. As Jeremiah prophesied in the name of the Lord about the coming day:

Keep your voice from weeping,
and your eyes from tears . . .
they shall come back from the land of the enemy.
There is hope for your future . . .
your children shall come back to their own country (31:16-17, RSV).

Isaiah 35 says that the children of God will come home singing. This is what Christmas can mean to us this year if we will open ourselves to God.

> This can be a time of coming home to God.
> This can be a time of opening ourselves to the
> Father's redemptive love.

This can be a time of repenting.
This can be a time of being forgiven.
This can be a season of being set free from
captivity to the forces of evil.
This can be a day of freedom and restoration at
the hands of the Prince of Peace.

We can come home again to God and sing and rejoice as we do so if we will but choose to do it! We must decide if we will allow this Advent and Christmas season to so bring us to the Father.

From his German prison cell, Nazi prisoner Dietrich Bonhoeffer wrote this letter to his parents right before their first Christmas apart:

From the Christian point of view there is no special problem about Christmas in a prison cell. For many people in this building it will probably be a more sincere and genuine occasion than in places where nothing but the name is kept. That misery, suffering, poverty, loneliness, helplessness, and guilt mean something quite different in the eyes of God from what they mean in the judgment of man, that God will approach where men turn away, that Christ was born in a stable because there was no room for him in the inn—these are things that a prisoner can understand better than other people; for him they are glad tidings, and that faith gives him a part in the communion of saints, a Christian fellowship breaking the bounds of time and space and reducing the months of confinement here to insignificance.[4]

I tell you during this Advent season, in light of what God has done for us in Jesus Christ, we should be weeping for the suffering of the children of the world and weeping for our sins against God and mankind. At this celebration of Christmas, we should be weeping for our lack of faith and lack of celebration of the good news of Jesus Christ. However, most of us weep only out of self-pity. Most of us lie awake only for anxiety over our hurt and loss or what we want more of. Where are your tears? Are you weeping genuinely for others?

When I am refinishing old furniture, the last part of the job is the least enjoyable, yet quite essential—and that is cleaning my varnish brush. To fail to clean the brush is to allow it to become hard and ruin. A casual cleaning is not enough. It must be cleaned in a cleaning solution, washed out with water, dried, and finally wrapped in a cloth for the next use. Many people do not keep their lives cleaned and ready for Christ to come in and use them. But as I found hope for renewing a brush not cleaned properly, there is hope for us. I have found a solution called a "brush restorer" which will help clean out old paint. It is never as good as new—the brush carries the scars of misuse—but it can be used again!

In the grace, mercy, love, forgiveness, and power of God in Christ Jesus we can be set free from our disabling captivity. We can be restored as children of the Father. We may carry the marks of our sin, but we can come home rejoicing, for we can experience a new relationship with God in a faith commitment in his strong Son, Jesus.

My wife's brother returned home safely though he had no guarantee of safety from the Marines. God guarantees us the gift of returning home to a joyous relationship with him. Where are your tears? Are you weeping for others? Are you weeping for yourself? Make room for Christ's lordship within your life, now!

Notes

1. Reprinted from FIDDLER ON THE ROOF by Joseph Stein. © 1964 by Joseph Stein. Music & Lyrics © 1964 by Sunbeam Music Corp. By permission of Crown Publishers Inc.

2. AP release, *Concord Tribune*, Dec. 10, 1979, p. 1.

3. " 'Saint of the Slums' Receives Nobel Prize," AP release, *Concord Tribune*, Dec. 10, 1979, p. 1.

4. *Letters and Papers from Prison*, Revised Edition by Dietrich Bonhoeffer (Copyright © 1953, 1967 by SCM Press Ltd.), p. 57.

Epiphany

Epiphany is the season that follows Christmas. In the coldest, darkest part of the year, this season holds forth the light and life of Jesus Christ to a lost and confused world. This is an evangelistic focus in worship, including in many denominations a Soul Winner's Commitment Sunday.

This order of worship begins with a quotation to call attention to the theme of salvation through grace. The headings of the segments of worship emphasize the thrust of this season of light. The statement prior to the last hymn is adapted from Dr. John R. Claypool, Jackson, Mississippi.

The congregation has the opportunity to participate in the summons to worship and the corporate benediction. On this day there is a congregational musical offertory response. The ushers wait at the back until the organist begins the initial chord of the song and then they come forward and place the plates on the altar during the singing.

THE WORSHIP OF GOD

SACRED ORGAN MUSIC

Conversion is turning away from sin toward God. The two elements are essential to each other and cannot be separated. When one genuinely turns away from sin, there is but one direction to turn: toward God. The converse is also true. One cannot turn toward God unless he has first turned away from sin. This is the deliberate act of will by which the individual turns his life from the direction he is traveling and redirects it toward God.

—C. B. Hogue

PRAISING THE GOD OF OUR SALVATION
CHIMING OF THE HOUR
SUMMONS TO WORSHIP

Leader: You chose to come here today when there are other places you could have gone and other things you could have done.

People: We have come here because we are seeking to be more authentic followers after Jesus the Christ. He calls us out of the world here to be a worshiping community, and then to go out again into the world as Christian witnesses.

Leader: Do you really feel this hour will accomplish anything of lasting significance?

People: We feel it will because we find it essential to bring our lives to the altar for prayer and offering and to encounter our fellow Christians to receive training, counsel, and encouragement.

Leader: Come, then, let us worship. Let us examine the way and life of Jesus the Christ whose invitation is simply and profoundly, "Follow Me."

HYMN   "Come, Thou Fount of Every Blessing"   Wyeth
INVOCATION
GREETING THE WORSHIPERS
ANTHEM

SEEING OURSELVES AS GOD SEES US
SCRIPTURE LESSON   Genesis 32:22-31
CALL TO PRAYER
PASTORAL PRAYER

GIVING WITNESS TO OUR COMMITMENT
HYMN   "Amazing Grace"   arr. by Excell

THE MORNING OFFERING
  Offertory Prayer
  Instrumental Offertory
  Offertory Response
    "Take my silver and my gold, / Not a mite would I withhold;
    Take my moments and my days,
    Let them flow in ceaseless praise."

PROCLAIMING THE NEWS OF OUR SALVATION
DUET
MESSAGE

RESPONDING TO THE GIFT OF GOD'S SALVATION
Listen—here is the Good News: "Christ Jesus came into the
world to save sinners"
  —to forgive you in your failure
  —to accept you as you are
  —to free you from evil's power and
    make you what you were created to be.
HYMN   "I Saw the Cross of Jesus"   Anonymous
PRESENTATION OF NEW MEMBERS
CORPORATE BENEDICTION

Leader: You said you came here for training, counsel,
          and encouragement. Now go and share the
          good news with others.
People: We will share the good news that God loves you
          and me,
Leader: And that Christ Jesus leads us to grace
People: So that we might realize and participate in his
          victory.
Leader: Amen,
People: And Amen.

Race Relations Sunday

Frequently it is difficult to speak an honest and helpful word on race relations in today's church. The potential for tension is high in some communities, so a resounding word from the Lord is needed on the subject.

The second section of this order of worship incorporates a musical expression of the Scriptures in Psalm 1 and a responsive reading of Paul's word on the subject in Galatians 3. The Psalms are called upon to stimulate private meditation prior to the pastoral prayer.

More than once a familiar hymn tune is used to enable the congregation to sing the words to an unfamiliar song. On this Sunday the words are printed so that the printed tune will not confuse the singing of a substituted tune. It is used by permission from *Seven Hymns of Concern and Ministry* (Nashville: Broadman Press, 1969), No. 6.

A litany for giving is used which originally appeared in the worship designed by Dr. John R. Claypool of the Northminster Baptist Church, Jackson, Mississippi.

THE WORSHIP OF GOD

SACRED INSTRUMENTAL MUSIC
 "A Mighty Fortress Is Our God"   arr. by Bauer
  Handbells
In fellowship with other like-minded folk, earnestly seeking to know and understand the will of God, comes the

practice of the presence of God. Their counsel, their experience, their questionings, their faith are the nourishment we need, the encouragement to keep on, the joy that delights us in knowing that we do not stand alone in our search.

—H. W. Freer and F. B. Hall

THE COMMUNITY OF FAITH GATHERS IN ONE ACCORD
OPENING SENTENCES
HYMN   "Ask Ye What Great Thing I Know"   Malan
INVOCATION
WELCOME TO THE WORSHIPERS

BREAKING THE BREAD OF LIFE
AND CONTINUING IN PRAYER
SINGING A MESSAGE OF DAVID
   Psalm 1   "Tree of Life"   Lee
      Youth Choir
READING AN EXPERIENCE OF PETER   Acts 10:1-23
READING A DECLARATION OF PAUL   Galatians 3:26-29 (RSV)

Leader: "For in Christ Jesus you are all sons of God,
          through faith.
People: For as many of you as were baptized into Christ
          have put on Christ.
Leader: There is neither Jew nor Greek,
People: There is neither slave nor free,
Leader: There is neither male nor female;
People: For you are all one in Christ Jesus.
Leader: And if you are Christ's, then you are Abraham's
          offspring, heirs according to promise."

SILENT PRAYER THOUGHTS

"Make me to know Thy ways, O Lord; teach me Thy paths.
Lead me in Thy truth, and teach me, for Thou art the God of
   my salvation.
Consider my affliction and my trouble, and forgive all my
   sins.

O guard my life, and deliver me; let me not be put to
  shame,
for I take refuge in Thee."
                                                  —Selected Psalms

PASTORAL PRAYER

THE CHRISTIAN COMMUNITY
SHARES ALL THINGS IN COMMON

HYMN   "Lord of Loving, Lord of Healing"
(Hymn: "What a Friend We Have in Jesus"; tune: CONVERSE)

Lord of loving, Lord of healing, Lord of merciful concern,
Teach us consecrated service to the helpless ones who
  yearn
For release from haunting hunger, sickness, loneliness,
  despair.
May we rise to concrete action; may we show them that we
  care.

To a populace exploding in its godless agony,
May we find new means of outreach, vision, sensitivity.
With a faith that is contagious—faith in Christ, whose min-
  istry
Was a personal involvement with a lost humanity.

From the pulpit, from the workshop, from the marketplace
  and lab,
To the suburb, to the city, slums so hostile, wretched,
  drab,
May Thy church accept the challenge of the needs of
  changing days,
That our service in Thy Spirit may turn hatred into praise.

To the insolent, the skeptic, those whose only law is hate,
Teach us how, O Lord, to love and serve and rehabilitate.
May we care with such abandon, such committed ministry,
That the words of Christ our Saviour may find hearts at-
  tuned to Thee.

MORNING OFFERING
  A Litany for Giving

Leader: Lord, teach us how to give,
People: So we will not embarrass those who cannot give
          as much,
Leader: Nor humiliate the ones to whom we give,
People: Nor give in order to take credit for ourselves.
Leader: Let us give as though we give directly to You, O
          God.
People: And be ashamed it is no more and that we do it
          no better.
Unison: Amen.

Organ Offertory   "Mine Eyes Are Unto Thee"   Price

THOUGHTFULLY HEARING THE WORD OF TRUTH
ANTHEM   "O Thou, to Whose All-Searching Sight"   Butler
                        Youth Choir
MESSAGE

AND THE LORD ADDS TO HIS CHURCH
HYMN   "I Surrender All"   Weeden
PRESENTATION OF NEW MEMBERS
PASTORAL BENEDICTION
CHORAL BENEDICTION "May the Road Rise to Meet You" Turner

    May the road rise to meet you,
    May the wind blow at your back,
    May the sun shine warmly on your face;
    May the rain fall softly on your field;
    And until we meet again, until we meet again,
    May God hold you in the palm of his hand. Amen.

ORGAN DISMISSAL   "Following Thee"   Frick

Lent

Lent is for Easter what Advent is for Christmas. For some unfortunate reasons, many churches have relegated the observance of Lent to the high church denominations and thus have failed to appreciate the rich resources of these six weeks of emphasis on self-discipline, cleansing, giving, and preparation for celebrating Easter.

Once a series of sermons was done during Lent, featuring the stained glass windows of the church's beautiful old sanctuary. The following order of worship was used the Sunday the focus was on the wheat window. The wheat lent itself to a dual focus on the interest in and importance of physical and spiritual food.

The congregation is provided a special time in this emphasis to confess their needs corporately, to silently confess their sins, and finally to hear words of forgiveness and assurance of pardon. The call to worship is adapted from First University United Methodist Church, Minneapolis, Minnesota, in *Ventures in Worship, Vol. I*, edited by David James Randolph. Copyright © 1969 by Abingdon Press, pp. 15-16. Used by permission.

THE WORSHIP OF GOD

SACRED ORGAN MUSIC

The worship of God in this place can be compared to a party for which God is the good host and to which everyone in his world is invited. Worship is the high celebration of the good news that we know the Creator of the universe and we have fellowship here on earth. Jesus expressed this truth in the parable of the great feast and our church at its best understands Christ himself to be the life of the party. This is a holy celebration. Use it wisely.

THE COMMUNITY OF FAITH GATHERS IN ONE ACCORD
SUMMONS TO WORSHIP
INVOCATION
HYMN   "Guide Me, O Thou Great Jehovah"   Hughes
GREETING THE WORSHIPERS

BREAKING THE BREAD OF LIFE
AND CONTINUING IN PRAYER
ANTHEM   "Jesus Our Lord We Adore Thee"   James
                               Choir
OLD TESTAMENT READING   Exodus 16:1-4,13-30
NEW TESTAMENT READING   John 6:25-40
CALL TO CONFESSION

Leader: Beloved, God has given us life, but we have often failed to live. We have been called to a way of freedom, but we have allowed ourselves to feel the burden is heavy and the anxiety painful and thus we have returned to our illusions about life and our deceits about ourselves. Let us admit what is really within our lives, for when we do, it will be given back to us with brand new meaning and fresh hope.

People: Spirit of life and love, come within us and fill us;

Leader: Spirit of grace and growth, move like a mighty wind to cleanse us;

People: Spirit of power and might, come as a fire to burn away our sinfulness;

Leader: Let us confess our sins.

SILENT CONFESSION OF SINS

PASTORAL PRAYER
WORDS OF ASSURANCE

THE COMMUNITY SHARES ALL THINGS IN COMMON
CHILDREN'S SERMON
HYMN   "Jesus, Thou Boundless Love to Me"   Hemy
THE MORNING OFFERING
   Offertory Prayer
   Handbell Offertory "Eternal Father, Strong to Save" Herbek
                              Handbells

THOUGHTFULLY HEARING THE WORD OF TRUTH
ANTHEM   "I Am the Bread of Life"   Roff
                                Choir
MESSAGE

THE LORD ADDS TO HIS CHURCH
HYMN   "Lord, Speak to Me, that I May Speak"   Schumann
PRESENTATION OF NEW MEMBERS
PASTORAL BENEDICTION
CHORAL RESPONSE   "Bread of Heaven"   Hastings
ORGAN DISMISSAL

Palm Sunday

This is a crucial Sunday in the life of the church. The preparation and anticipation of Easter is high on this day. Everything should point toward the willingness of Christ's deed and the necessity of our committed discipleship.

A printed prayer appears at the beginning of the order of worship as an attempt to focus the worshipers' attention on the vital theme of the day. On a day of palm branches and celebration, handbells are used and a procession of children with palm branches is included during the opening hymn. A cross is in place at the front of the sanctuary. The children lay their branches around the base of the cross. This cross appears from Palm Sunday through Easter Sunday, using a crown of thorns prior to Easter and a crown triumphant on Easter morning.

The worshipers have three additional ways to participate in the worship experience on this day. They may join in a responsive call to worship, sing an additional hymn as a congregational musical call to prayer, and enter into the responsive corporate benediction.

The headings for this Sunday pull together the theme of the day. Emphasis is placed on the importance of commitment on Palm Sunday.

The prayer thought is adapted from James Weakley in *Ventures in Worship, Vol. II*, edited by David James Randolph, Copyright © 1970 by Abingdon Press, p. 141. Used by permission. The benediction is adapted from one by John Curtis in *Ventures in Worship Vol. III*, edited by David James Ran-

THE WORSHIP OF GOD

Our Father God, we gather in your presence with many emotions. We are flooded with confusion . . . disappointment . . . sadness . . . doubt . . . guilt . . . shame . . . spite . . . prejudice . . . bitterness . . . grief . . . envy . . . . We never seem able to internalize your wisdom in our living for these days. We continually drift back into the same sins which we attempt but never quite conquer. What do we lack . . . insight . . . faith . . . consistency . . . desire . . . courage . . . boldness?

We stand here on this day of palm branches and hosannas with dust in our eyes and mouths, for we are ashamed to hail you as the King of our hearts while we are living in the midst of a materialistic world—and perhaps even in this very room! With gratitude we recall that you sent your Son to forgive unworthy, sinful people such as we are. We ask you to be merciful to us who flounder in our sea of mixed motives and unresolved commitments. We ask you to

> help us desire forgiveness and strength . . . which you offer us now
>
> help us respond to your challenge to serve . . . as you have served
>
> help us be willing to forgive our enemies . . . as you have forgiven us
>
> compel us to love the unlovely . . . as you have loved us.

SACRED HANDBELL MUSIC

PRAISING THE NAME OF GOD

OPENING SENTENCES

Leader: Good morning!
People: Good morning!

Leader: I am pleased to welcome you to this celebration of worship in the Father's House.

People: We have come to seek for new truth and to search for new meaning.

Leader: Jesus said, "I have come to seek and to save those who are lost."

People: He has motivated our coming, for we want to know him and his ways, that they might become our own ways.

Leader: Open your ears, your mind, and your heart to encounter him, for he is here!

People: We are opening ourselves and we do sense he is here with us!

Unison: Praise the Lord! He is here! We will worship him completely!

INVOCATION
PROCESSIONAL   "Glorious Is Thy Name"   McKinney
GREETING THE WORSHIPERS
ANTHEM

COMMUNING WITH THE SPIRIT OF GOD
READING OF THE WORD   Mark 14:32-42
CONGREGATIONAL CALL TO PRAYER
  HYMN   "O Sacred Head, Now Wounded"   Bach
PASTORAL PRAYER
ANTHEM

OFFERING GIFTS IN THE NAME OF GOD
HYMN   "Christian Hearts, in Love United"
(Hymn. "What a Friend We Have in Jesus"; tune: CONVERSE)
THE MORNING OFFERING
  Offertory Sentences
  Handbell Offertory

DECLARING THE MESSAGE OF REDEMPTION
SOLO
MESSAGE

RESPONDING WITH THE COMMITMENT OF LIFE
HYMN   "Beneath the Cross of Jesus"   Maker
PRESENTATION OF NEW MEMBERS
CORPORATE BENEDICTION

Leader: Go, and prepare yourself for the cross and the crucifixion.
People: May we love the Lord our God with all our heart.
Leader: Go, and seek to serve as one who knows the resurrection.
People: May we love our neighbor as ourselves.
Leader: Amen.
People: And Amen.

ORGAN DISMISSAL

Easter

Easter is probably one of the easiest Sundays to muster enthusiasm for. Not only is it a time of joy but also it is a Sunday the sanctuary is filled!

This Sunday has extra music, both by the choir and by the congregation who sing one familiar hymn as the congregational musical call to worship.

The headings draw attention to the fact that Easter is about light, reality, giving, and faith. Newness came and will come again to those open to God's moving in our midst. The poem comes from Dr. John R. Claypool, Broadway Baptist Church, Fort Worth, Texas. The Easter Litany is adapted from one by Norman C. Habel, *Interrobang* (Philadelphia: Fortress Press, 1969), p. 82. Used by permission.

The litany allows the worshipers to express in a safe, corporate manner some of the questions and feelings they are having. This is one of the important features of responsive readings. People can greatly benefit by saying something of personal, theological importance out loud together that might never be said alone.

With additional music planned on this day, care must be taken to start on time and preach a bit shorter sermon in order to adjourn the large congregation promptly!

THE WORSHIP OF GOD

God, I'm scared!
It's grim in this gully—

mountainous ruts all around—
can't see a thing.

My salt is savorless,
my pearls worthless,
my light about
to flicker out . . .

What?
You want me to climb that bald hill
to a splintery old cross—
share Godview with You?

Say,
things do look different from up here.
There's even enough light to see
that the cross is empty,
the tomb bare.

—Beverly Hill

FROM DARKNESS TO LIGHT

CHORAL PRELUDE "All Hail the Power of Jesus' Name" Galbraith
Soloist and Choir
CONGREGATIONAL CALL TO WORSHIP
"Low in the Grave He Lay"   Lowry

Low in the grave he lay, Jesus my Savior!
Waiting the coming day, Jesus my Lord!

Vainly they watch his bed, Jesus my Savior!
Vainly they seal the dead, Jesus my Lord!

Death cannot keep his prey, Jesus my Savior!
He tore the bars away, Jesus my Lord!

Up from the grave he arose, With a mighty triumph o'er His
foes;
He arose a victor from the dark domain,
And he lives forever with his saints to reign.
He arose! He arose! Hallelujah! Christ arose!

INVOCATION
HYMN   "Christ the Lord Is Risen Today"   Davidica
GREETING THE WORSHIPERS

FROM PROMISE TO REALITY
AN EASTER LITANY

Leader: People of God, why do you seek the living among the dead?

People: Because we are afraid, we are uncertain, we are uncomfortable here, and we have doubts about Jesus Christ.

Leader: Do not be afraid, for he has risen from the dead, he has broken through the tomb, he has come back to life, and he is here among us now! People of God, why do you seek the living among the dead?

People: Because we feel guilty, we feel lonely, and we feel lost, for we, too, have deserted Christ.

Leader: Do not carry your guilt any longer, for he has taken the guilt himself, he has buried it in his grave, he has lifted it to his cross, and he is here among us now. People of God, why do you seek the living among the dead?

People: Because our wounds are deep. We have torn away from Christ, we have broken with him and with our fellowmen.

Leader: Do not dwell on your wounds for he has risen to heal you, he has risen to forgive you, he has risen to change you all and bind us all together now. People of God, Christ is not in the grave—he is risen!

People: Yes, he is risen!

Unison: Thanks be to our Almighty God! He is risen!

ANTHEM   "Alleluia, Come, Good People"   Davis
                              Choir

AN EASTER PRAYER

FROM RECEIVING TO GIVING
HYMN   "The First Lord's Day"   Baptist Hymnal
    (Hymn: "At the Cross"; tune: HUDSON)
MORNING OFFERING
    Offertory Prayer
    Handbell Offertory   "Easter Meditation"   Vulpius
                              Handbells

FROM DOUBT TO FAITH
ANTHEM   "But Now Is Christ Risen"   Peterson
                Choir
READING OF THE WORD   Mark 16:1-8
MESSAGE
HYMN   "Ask Ye What Great Thing I Know"   Malan
PRESENTATION OF NEW MEMBERS
BENEDICTION
ORGAN DISMISSAL   "In Joyful Praise"   Martin

Low Sunday

Some people have come to believe that Low Sunday is so named because the Sunday after Easter has such lower attendance than the previous Sunday. The name and tradition of this day comes rather from the fact that after reaching a mountaintop religious experience, we tend to have a letdown not unlike Elijah leaving Mount Carmel. Of course, it may be this letdown that precipitates the decline in attendance!

The congregation is asked to participate in two responsive readings—the opening sentences and the parting declaration of faith, and two musical responses—to the offertory and to the benediction. The opening sentences are adapted from Dr. John R. Claypool, Broadway Baptist Church, Fort Worth, Texas. The third hymn is reprinted by permission from *Seven Hymns of Concern and Ministry* (Nashville: Broadman Press, 1969), No. 3.

The headings emphasize Christ's lordship even on a Low Sunday. The quotation at the top of the order of worship gives further focus on the centrality of the theme.

THE WORSHIP OF GOD

Sacred Organ Music
"The word Lord is a one-word creed, a one-word expression of complete devotion, a one-word expression of reverence and adoration. There is little wonder that it was the

word in which the Church summed up its belief in Jesus Christ, and one of the Church's most claimant needs today is the rediscovery of its meaning, and the cessation of the empty use of the greatest name of Jesus Christ."

—William Barclay

CROWN CHRIST LORD OF ALL
OPENING SENTENCES

Leader: In the name of Jesus and in the spirit of community, I call you to the celebration of worship.

People: We come to join together in this place of worship,
to affirm we are Christ's church,
to lift up our lives, words, and thoughts,
so as to make this time together a celebration of worship.

Leader: The Spirit of the Lord is upon us. He has called us to this time and place and to this life of love and service.

People: We accept his call and gather here to renew our lives and make fresh our loyalties.

Leader: Let us revitalize our commitment of living and loving taught by Jesus Christ our Lord.

People: Jesus Christ is our Lord! To him be praise and glory!

HYMN   "O Church of God, Triumphant"   Smart
INVOCATION
WELCOME TO THE WORSHIPERS
ANTHEM

AFFIRM HIM AS LORD OF THE PAST AND FUTURE
CHILDREN'S SERMON
OLD TESTAMENT LESSON   Isaiah 43:14-21
NEW TESTAMENT LESSON   Romans 13:11-14
MORNING PRAYER

ACKNOWLEDGE HIM AS LORD
THROUGH SELFLESS GIVING

HYMN   "Christian Men, Arise and Give"   Kocher

MORNING OFFERING

Offertory Prayer

Handbell Offertory "Meditation on C and F Bells" Burroughs

Offertory Response   "Glorious Is Thy Name Most Holy"

(Hymn: "Joyful, Joyful, We Adore Thee"; tune: HYMN TO JOY)

For our world of need and anguish we would lift to thee our
prayer.

Faithful stewards of thy bounty, May we with our brothers
share.

In the name of Christ our Savior, Who redeems and sets us
free,

Gifts we bring of heart and treasure, That our lives may
worthier be.

DECLARE HIM AS LORD OF OUR PRESENT DAY

SOLO

MESSAGE

HYMN   "Lord, Lead Thy Church"
            (Hymn: "Just As I Am"; tune: WOODWORTH)

Lord, lead thy church to be renewed by selfless covenant,
we pray.

To serve our world as thou wouldst do, to lift its load day
after day.

Have mercy on the hungry horde who starve where fields
are waste and drear.

We break the loaf of bread we've stored to feed our
brothers far and near.

From suburb and from squalid slum ascend the cries of
deep despair.

Lord, stir our hearts to need grown numb, to love and
hopeless everywhere.

Lord, heal our blindness. May we see thy image stamped
on everyone.

For thou hast said, "It's unto me your service to the least is
done."

PRESENTATION OF NEW MEMBERS
A PARTING DECLARATION OF FAITH

Leader: As we depart, let us do so with a certainty about
          our faith. What is the witness of the Scripture
          concerning Jesus of Nazareth?
People: Jesus Christ is Lord!
Leader: What has been the witness of the faithful
          through the ages?
People: Jesus Christ is Lord!
Leader: What is your declaration of faith?
People: Jesus Christ is Lord!

CONGREGATIONAL RESPONSE
"They Will Know We Are Christian by Our Love"
ORGAN DISMISSAL

Christian Home Week

The first Sunday of the eight-day Christian Home Week is an important day to deal with interpersonal relationships in the family. Generation gaps, sexual gaps, sibling gaps, in-law gaps, career gaps, and many other gaps rear their heads before the modern family.

The congregation is afforded the opportunity to participate in the call to worship and the offertory response. The spoken response is concluded with the "Doxology."

Senior adults are recognized on this day. A contemporary reading is included along with Old and New Testament readings. The parallelism of "Through . . ." is repeated five times in the sections entitled "He Spoke *Through* Our Fathers" and "He Speaks *Through* Us."

THE WORSHIP OF GOD

God delights in all who worship on this Lord's Day!
From different places and from different walks of life
you have come to share this time of worship. Our
prayer is that the Holy Spirit will so unite us that we
shall become one worshiping body seeking
to know and to do our Lord's will.

WE GATHER BEFORE THE GOD WHO MADE US

SACRED ORGAN MUSIC
CORPORATE CALL TO WORSHIP

Leader: For all the greatness of God's creativity,
People: We express our joy and thanksgiving.
Leader: For all the goodness of God's loving mercy.
People: We express our joy and thanksgiving.
Leader: For all the strength of God's abiding presence,
People: We express our joy and thanksgiving.
Leader: Because we affirm our joy for what God has
          done for us, let us worship him joyfully with our
          whole beings!

INVOCATION
HYMN   "To Worship, Work, and Witness"   Webb
GREETING OF WORSHIPERS AND RECOGNITION OF SENIOR ADULTS
ANTHEM   "Great Is Thy Faithfulness"   Runyan
                          Choir

HE SPOKE THROUGH OUR FATHERS
THROUGH THE OLD TESTAMENT   Genesis 12:1-8
THROUGH THE NEW TESTAMENT   Luke 2:41-52

HE SPEAKS THROUGH US
THROUGH A CONTEMPORARY READING
   "Only Children"   Kathryn R. Deering
THROUGH A CHORAL MEDITATION
THROUGH A PRAYER

IN HIM WE LIVE AND MOVE
HYMN   "Show, O Lord, Thy Blessed Face"
          (Hymn: "Holy Bible, Book Divine"; tune: ALETTA)
MORNING OFFERING
   Offertory Prayer
   Handbell Offertory
      "All Creatures of Our God and King"   arr. by Scoggins
                       Handbells
   Offertory Response

Leader: Every man shall give as he is able, according to
          the blessing of the Lord our God which he has
          given us.

People: We give of ourselves and our resources, as God
           has blessed us.
Leader: Then let us "Praise God, from Whom All Bless-
           ings Flow":
           "Praise God, from whom all blessings flow;
           Praise him all creatures here below;
           Praise him above, ye heav'nly host;
           Praise Father, Son, and Holy Ghost. Amen."

HE OFFERS NEW LIFE TO US

ANTHEM
MESSAGE
HYMN   "Jesus Is All the World to Me"   Thompson
PRESENTATION OF NEW MEMBERS
SPOKEN BENEDICTION
CHORAL BENEDICTION
ORGAN DISMISSAL

Parent-Baby Dedication Sunday

The other end of Christian Home Week is a celebration of the dedication of parents and church to help nurture newborn children in the knowledge of Jesus Christ. There is no membership in the church involved, there is no water used, and there are no magical words! This is an occasion of affirming the family and assuring the church's involvement in Christian growth of the family.

A special dedication litany is provided for the parents and church to express their seriousness and commitment to the task of rearing the children God has bestowed upon them. The congregation also has an opportunity to participate in the opening sentences and the benediction. The opening sentences are adapted from a writing of Ronald A. Houk in *Ventures in Worship, Vol. II,* edited by David James Randolph. Copyright © 1970 by Abingdon Press, p. 54. Used by permission.

THE WORSHIP OF GOD

GOD'S CHILDREN GATHER
SACRED ORGAN MUSIC

TO AFFIRM HIS PRESENCE
WELCOME TO THE WORSHIPERS
OPENING SENTENCES

Leader: Good morning!

People: Good morning!
Leader: It is a good morning in Jesus Christ. Every day is exciting and fresh in him.
People: We have come to worship and praise him who makes every day new and all of life joyful.
Leader: Then let us show our gratitude to Jesus the Christ, the One who makes all of life an adventure in meaning and purpose.

CHORAL CALL TO WORSHIP
INVOCATION
HYMN "God Give Us Christian Homes" McKinney

TO DEDICATE PARENTS AND BABIES TO HIM
ADDRESS TO THE PARENTS
COVENANT OF DEDICATION

Leader: Do you recognize your responsibility as parents and do you bring your child here in dedication to God in the presence of this church as a sign of your dependence on divine help to fulfill your parental duties?
Parents: We do.
Leader: Do you solemnly commit yourselves to seek to bring up your child in the nurture and knowledge of God?
Parents: We do.
Leader: Do you commit yourselves to use all the resources available to teach and lead your child both to experience a personal relationship with Christ and to develop a Christ-like character?
Parents: We do.
Leader: Do you faithfully commit yourselves to try to provide the home life and the church experience that will shape the kind of environment that will enable your child to profess Christ as Lord and serve him as Master?
Parents: We do.
Leader: If you, the church, realize your responsibility to

help in providing the kind of environment that
will point children to Christ and help them to
grow in the life God intends, will you rise? Do
you commit yourselves to seek to fulfill your
responsibility?

People: *We do.*

PRAYER OF DEDICATION
PRESENTATION OF THE CHILDREN
(Names of babies born in last twelve months and their
parents are printed here.)
BLESSING
HYMN   "Friend of the Home"
                (Hymn: "Abide with Me"; tune: EVENTIDE)
Friend of the home, as when, in Galilee,
The mothers brought their little ones to Thee,
So we, dear Lord, would now the children bring,
And seek for them the shelter of Thy wing.

Lord, may Thy church, as with a mother's care,
For Thee the lambs within her bosom bear;
And grant, as morning grows to noon, that they
Still in her love and holy service stay.

Draw, through the child, the parents nearer Thee,
Endue their home with growing sanctity;
And gather all, by earthly homes made one,
In heaven, O Christ, when earthly days are done.

THE MORNING OFFERING
  Offertory Sentences
  Piano Duet   "Jesus Loves Me"   arr. by Kraus

TO COMMIT OURSELVES TO THE FATHER
ANTHEM
SCRIPTURE READING   Genesis 2:18-24; Mark 10:2-12
MESSAGE
HYMN   "Lord, I Want to Be a Christian"   Work
PRESENTATION OF NEW MEMBERS

GOD'S CHILDREN DEPART

CORPORATE BENEDICTION

Leader: We have worshiped together. We cannot remain here. Now we must depart to go into the Father's world.

People: We will encounter need in every dimension of life—in our homes, on our jobs, in our recreation.

Leader: The world longs to know the good news of our love and joy in Christ Jesus.

People: Let us accept our mission to share Christ with each person we encounter, leading them to know the joy of his salvation.

Leader: May it be so with each of us.

People: May it be so.

Leader: Amen.

ORGAN DISMISSAL

TO LIVE HIS WILL IN CHRISTIAN HOMES

Memorial Sunday

The holiday weekend enables many families to travel for Memorial Sunday. With two options of when to remember the members who have died during the last year—this Sunday or Reformation Sunday—the ease of travel leans toward this Sunday.

A personal letter reminds each family that the name of their loved one who died will be read during a memorial service on this day. The section headings are drawn from Psalm 23 and lend strength and encouragement to bereaved families.

The congregation has the opportunity to engage in the summons to worship and the unison benediction. The invocation is sung by the congregation.

With so much anxiety about life and death, the sermon for this Sunday should focus on affirming a Christian stance on facing life and death in the power and strength of Christ through the Holy Spirit.

THE WORSHIP OF GOD
SACRED ORGAN MUSIC

REMEMBERING GOD, THE GOOD SHEPHERD, IS WITH US
SUMMONS TO WORSHIP

Leader: We gather to celebrate God's gift of new life in Jesus Christ,

People: Both to receive our lives as gifts and to offer them to God as gifts.

Leader: We gather to remember in gratitude,
People: Both to say thanks for what has been and to say yes to what will be.
Leader: We gather to anticipate in hope,
People: Both to affirm the promises we have received and to live with the assurance of what is to come.
Leader: We gather to worship God,
People: Both to honor him as the worthy One and the One who gives each of us unique worth.

CONGREGATIONAL INVOCATION   (Hymn: "My Jesus, I Love Thee"; tune: GORDON)

Our Father in heaven, we hallow thy name;
May thy kingdom holy on earth be the same:
O give to us daily our portion of bread:
It is from thy bounty that all must be fed.

Forgive our transgressions, and teach us to know
That humble compassion which pardons each foe;
Keep us from temptation, from evil and sin,
And thine be the glory, forever! Amen!

GREETING THE WORSHIPERS
HYMN   "Teach Me, O Lord, I Pray"   Elvey
CHILDREN'S SERMON

EVEN IN THE VALLEY OF DEATH

A MEMORIAL SERVICE
(Names of members who died in the last twelve months are printed here.)
THE MEMORIAL PRAYER
SOLO

HE FURNISHES OUR TABLE BOUNTIFULLY

HYMN   "Sweet Hour of Prayer"   Bradbury
THE MORNING OFFERING
   Offertory Prayer
   Organ Offertory "O Christ, Who Art the Light and Day" Bach

HIS GOODNESS AND MERCY FOLLOW US ALWAYS

ANTHEM
READING OF THE WORD   Revelation 3:15-22
MESSAGE
HYMN   "Have Thine Own Way, Lord"   Stebbins
PRESENTATION OF NEW MEMBERS

AND WE SHALL ABIDE IN HIS FELLOWSHIP FOREVER

CORPORATE BENDICTION
  Unison: Father, strengthen us so that the winds of the
            world will never dim the flame you have lit in our
            hearts. Amen.
ORGAN DISMISSAL

Trinity Sunday

This Sunday, which follows Pentecost Sunday, marks the beginning of the second "half" of the Christian Year. This is the beginning of the period in which emphasis might well be placed on the teachings of Jesus. It is important at the outset to focus with clarity on the threefold revelation of God to man through himself as Father/Creator, Son/Savior, and Spirit/Companion. A lot of unsettled questions remain in most Protestant churches because little preaching and teaching are offered in the area of the Holy Spirit and the Triune revelation of God.

A statement to direct attention on the theme of the Trinity appears at the outset of this worship guide. The congregation is provided three unique opportunities for involvement in worship through the musical call to worship, the responsive call to prayer, and the corporate choral benediction. Both of the musical pieces should be familiar before using them at such crucial places in the morning worship.

The hymns are selected to tie in the Trinity theme. The headings for the sections of the worship are designed to draw attention to the theme of God's movement among us through his Triune revelation.

THE WORSHIP OF GOD

SACRED ORGAN MUSIC

SPIRIT OF THE LIVING GOD

Let us attempt to affirm on this Trinity Sunday that God has made himself known to us in three ways—
The loving Father who breathes into us daily the gift of life
The redeeming Son who provides for us the gift of salvation with eternal life and
The companion Spirit whose gift of abiding presence sustains us throughout life.

CONGREGATIONAL CALL TO
HYMN   "Spirit of the Living God"   McKinney

Spirit of the living God, fall fresh on me;
Spirit of the living God, fall fresh on me.
Break me, melt me, mold me, fill me.
Spirit of the living God, fall fresh on me.

INVOCATION
HYMN   "God, Our Father, We Adore Thee"   Zundel

DESCEND UPON THY CHURCH ONCE MORE

ANTHEM
OLD TESTAMENT READING   Ezekiel 36:26-27
NEW TESTAMENT READING   Acts 4:31-36
CALL TO PRAYER

Leader: May our prayers be for the understanding that God sends his Holy Spirit to abide within the members of this church,
People: To give us light for dark problems,
Leader: Comfort for times of pain and grief,
People: In order that we may be guided through the mazes of our complex, troubled lives.
Leader: God has assured us as believers that he will not leave us alone. So, my friends, in him claim his promise for you today.
Unison: Come, Holy Spirit;
come in your great power and glory upon this Christ's Church; come bring us

a new birth of righteousness,
a new understanding of truth,
a new concept of our mission, and
a new unity in love.

MORNING PRAYER

FILL IT WITH LOVE AND JOY AND POWER
HYMN   "Thou, Whose Purpose Is to Kindle"
(Hymn: "Jesus Calls Us O'er the Tumult" tune: GALILEE)
MORNING OFFERING
Offertory Prayer
Instrumental Offertory

TILL CHRIST SHALL REIGN IN HUMAN HEARTS
ANTHEM
MESSAGE
CALL TO DISCIPLESHIP
HYMN   "Breathe on Me"   McKinney
PRESENTATION OF NEW MEMBERS
GREETING THE VISTORS
CORPORATE BENEDICTION
"There's a Sweet, Sweet Spirit in This Place"

Children's Sunday

Somewhere in all the hustle and bustle about Mother's Day and Father's Day, most children feel left out. A tradition that has not caught on in many churches has determined midway between the parents' days is Children's Sunday—the second Sunday in June.

This Sunday's worship allows the congregation to join in a unison call to worship from the Psalms and to engage in a responsive benediction. The section headings focus on God the Father and us the children.

Worship leaders are regularly used. On this Sunday two children may be chosen for the worship leaders. The worship leaders read responsively the Scripture passages assigned to them.

THE WORSHIP OF GOD

SACRED ORGAN MUSIC

The saint is one who knows that every moment of our human life is a moment of crisis; for at every moment we are called upon to make an all-important decision—to choose between the way that leads to death and spiritual darkness and the way that leads to light and life; between interests exclusively temporal and the eternal order; between our personal will or the will of some projection of our personality, and the will of God.

—A. Huxley

PRAISING THE FATHER OF ALL
CORPORATE CALL TO WORSHIP

Unison: "God be gracious to us and bless us
and make his face to shine upon us,
that thy way may be known upon earth,
thy saving power among all nation."
—Psalm 67:1-2

HYMN   "For the Beauty of the Earth"   Kocher
INVOCATION
GREETING THE WORSHIPERS
ANTHEM

REMEMBERING WE ARE CHILDREN
RESPONSIVE READING
The Scriptures and Children   Isaiah 11:6; Mark 10:14;
Ecclesiastes 12:1; Luke 18:17; Proverbs 22:6; 20:11; 1 Timothy 4:12; Ephesians 6:1
ANTHEM
MORNING PRAYER

RETURNING THE GIFTS TO THE FATHER
HYMN   "With Happy Voices Ringing"
(Hymn: "The Church's One Foundation"; tune: AURELIA)

"With happy voices ringing, Thy children, Lord, appear;
Their joyous praises bringing in anthems full and clear;
For skies of golden splendor, For azure rolling sea,
For blossoms sweet and tender, O Lord, we worship Thee.

For though no eye beholds Thee, No hand Thy touch may
feel,
Thy universe unfolds Thee, Thy starry heav'ns reveal;
The earth and all its glory, Our homes and all we love
Tell forth the wondrous story Of One who reigns above.

And shall we not adore Thee, With more than joyous song,
And live in truth before Thee, All beautiful and strong?
Lord, bless our souls' endeavor Thy servants true to be,
And through all life, forever, To live our praise to Thee."

MORNING OFFERING
Offertory Prayer
Invitation to Giving
Giving is the natural consequence of loving.
Let the gifts we offer the Father reflect the love we bear.
Organ Offertory

HEARING THE WORD OF THE FATHER
MESSAGE

EXPRESSING COMMITMENT TO THE FATHER
HYMN   "I Have Decided to Follow Jesus"   arr. by Reynolds
PRESENTATION OF NEW MEMBERS
CONGREGATIONAL BENEDICTION

Leader: O Lord, the Source of life and Giver of abun-
         dant life, we thank you for the experiences of
         this hour.
People: We will seek to express our thanksgiving by the
         manner in which we live out our growing com-
         mitment to Christ's lordship during these days.
Leader: So may it be.
People: Amen.

ORGAN DISMISSAL

Christian Citizenship Sunday

Frequently religion and patriotism appear to be so entwined that they are indistinguishable. The other danger is that as American Christians we will so neglect to exercise our Christian citizenship that we might lose our freedoms—including the freedom to worship.

The worship planned for this day allows the church to express its loyalty to the American flag, the Christian flag, and the Bible—something most adults have not done since Vacation Bible School days! The congregation also is able to join in the power of 2 Chronicles 7:14 through the thoughtful call to prayer.The initial ringing is done on chimes or handbells to signal the hour of worship.

Worship on such a day must not merge Christian faith into civil religion, but it can afford an inspiring hour for all the people.

THE WORSHIP OF GOD

RECOGNIZING OUR FREEDOM

Remember always that all of us, and you and I especially, are descended from immigrants and revolutionists.
—Franklin D. Roosevelt, 1938

RINGING FREEDOM'S SONG
PLEDGE OF ALLEGIANCE TO THE AMERICAN FLAG

I pledge allegiance to the flag of the United States of America,

and to the republic for which it stands,
one nation under God, indivisible,
with liberty and justice for all.

INVOCATION
CELEBRATING AMERICA'S FREEDOM
GREETING THE WORSHIPERS

ASKING GOD TO MAKE US FREE

HYMN   "My Country, 'Tis of Thee"   Anonymous
PLEDGE OF ALLEGIANCE TO THE CHRISTIAN FLAG

I pledge allegiance to the Christian flag,
and to the Savior for whose kingdom it stands,
one brotherhood uniting all Christians in service and love.

PLEDGE OF ALLEGIANCE TO THE BIBLE

I pledge allegiance to the Bible, God's holy Word,
and will make it a lamp unto my feet, a light unto my path,
and hide its words in my heart that I may not sin against
    God.

READING OF THE WORD   Matthew 22:15-22
CALL TO PRAYER

Leader: "If my people who are called by my name . . ."
People: Help us, O Lord, to remember who we are.
Leader: "Humble themselves . . ."
People: Help us, O Lord, to realize who we are.
Leader: "And pray and seek my face . . ."
People: Help us, O Lord, to recognize who you are.
Leader: "And turn from their wicked ways . . ."
People: Help us, O Lord, to recall who we were meant to
           be.
Leader: "Then I will hear from heaven, and will forgive
           their sin and heal their land" (2 Chron. 7:14,
           RSV).
People: Help us, O Lord, to allow you to forgive us, heal
           us, and make us free.

PRAYER FOR FREEDOM

RETURNING OUR GIFTS IN FREEDOM

HYMN   "O God of Our Fathers"   arr. by Kremser
MORNING OFFERING
   Offertory Prayer
   Organ Offertory

SEEKING FREEDOM WITHIN

ANTHEM
MESSAGE
HYMN   "God Calling Yet! Shall I Not Hear?"   Bradbury

"God calling yet! shall I not hear? Earth's pleasures shall I
   still hold dear?
Shall life's swift passing years all fly, And still my soul in
   slumber lie?
God calling yet! and shall he knock, And I my heart the
   closer lock?
He still is waiting to receive, And shall I dare his Spirit
   grieve?
God calling yet! and shall I give No heed, but still in bond-
   age live?
I wait, but he does not forsake; He calls me still! my heart,
   awake!
God calling yet! I cannot stay; My heart I yield without
   delay:
Vain world, farewell; from thee I part; The voice of God
   hath reach'd my heart."

PRESENTATION OF NEW MEMBERS
BENEDICTION
CHORAL RESPONSE
ORGAN DISMISSAL

Labor Day Sunday

While there is no theological significance to this national holiday, Labor Day does provide a fitting occasion to focus on the need for Christian laborers. Most people's minds will be geared to working in the world; therefore, this is an appropriate hour to pull their attention back to the truth that as Christians they are to labor in the world as well as in the church in Christ's name.

The guide to worship is illustrative of what can be written by the local minister to help draw the congregation to a mood for genuine worship. The statement of affirmation is adapted from an earlier statement by Dr. John R. Claypool of Jackson, Mississippi.

Once again, an unfamiliar hymn is suggested to be sung to a familiar tune. Words are never printed without copyright permission *or* sufficient books in the church that the congregation could have sung from their own books. It is permissible to print the words to simplify the singing as long as books are available. "O Master Workman of the Race" was written by Jay T. Stocking.

The benediction is a musical corporate one.

THE WORSHIP OF GOD

SACRED ORGAN MUSIC

This hour of worship can become a flat, empty time when

mind and emotions are put in neutral. Out of habit, sense of obligation, or pressure from family or peers, we may come to a holy place for wrong reasons. God has created us with the desire and potential for communion with him. This hour is designed to provide each of us the unique opportunity of worshiping God corporately. Rejoice in the presence of God. Remember that others have come here to worship. Realize an authentic, personal reason for being in this place.

—Robert W. Bailey

SAYING WHO WE ARE

CHIMING OF THE HOUR
STATEMENT OF AFFIRMATION

Leader: As we begin the worship of God, let us affirm who we are.

People: We are laborers. We have all invested a goodly portion of our time in the work we have chosen to do, and we have come to this place for rest and strength.

Leader: God himself ordained this pattern. In the very shaping of the world, he toiled and then he rested. Who else are we?

People: We are co-laborers in the kingdom of our Lord. We work together with those around us, and we are fellow workmen with God.

Leader: We join hands with the apostle Paul who collaborated with God in the significant task of spreading the gospel. Who else are we?

People: We are ministers. The quality of our work matters to us, but it is the means of our living so that we can respond to our divine calling. Ministry in Christ's name is our basic calling.

Leader: Jesus of Nazareth is our supreme example. He worked as a carpenter, yet ever keeping in mind the larger work of redemption to which his life was given. Let us strive to be like him.

HYMN   "Lead on, O King Eternal"   Smart
INVOCATION
WELCOME TO THE WORSHIPERS
ANTHEM

ACKNOWLEDGING OUR NEEDFULNESS
OLD TESTAMENT READING   Psalm 127:1-2
NEW TESTAMENT READING   Luke 10:1-2
PASTORAL PRAYER

OFFERING OUR GIFTS
HYMN   "O Master Workman of the Race"
(Hymn: "America the Beautiful" tune: MATERNA)

"O Master Workman of the race, Thou Man of Galilee,
Who, with the eyes of early youth, Eternal things didst see;
We thank Thee for Thy boyhood faith That shone Thy
    whole life through:
'Did ye not know it is my work my Father's work to do?'

O Carpenter of Nazareth, Builder of life divine,
Who shapest man to God's own law, Thyself the fair de-
    sign,
Build us a tow'r of Christ-like height, That we the land may
    view,
And see, like Thee, our noblest work, Our Father's work to
    do.

O Thou who dost the vision send, And givest each his task,
And with the task sufficient strength: Show us Thy will, we
    ask;
Give us a conscience bold and good; Give us a purpose
    true,
That it may be our highest joy Our Father's work to do."

THE MORNING OFFERING
Offertory Prayer
Organ Offertory

HEARING THE WORD OF GOD
CHORAL MEDITATION
MESSAGE

RESPONDING IN FAITH

HYMN   "God of Grace and God of Glory"   Hughes
PRESENTATION OF NEW MEMBERS
CORPORATE BENEDICTION   Hughes
"Grant us wisdom, Grant us courage,
That we fail not man nor thee!
That we fail not man nor thee! Amen."
ORGAN DISMISSAL

Deacon Ordination/ Installation

One of the very special days in the life of a church is the ordination of new deacons and the installation of other elected deacons. This order of worship presents the usual opening of worship, including a responsive call to worship.

The fourth section illustrates the recognition of the deacons and a covenant between the minister and deacons and finally the church. The direct part with the deacons is concluded with the affirmation of ordination and installation.

Careful planning as to positioning of the new deacon, the availability of microphones, and the advance purchase of gift books for the deacons will help make this a very special day, indeed. Unless the worship event will exceed an hour, some time will have to be trimmed off the sermon!

The call to worship is adapted from Dr. John R. Claypool, Broadway Baptist Church, Fort Worth, Texas.

THE WORSHIP OF GOD

Here we stand, as an innumerable company before us have stood, at the last outpost of human endeavor, seeking God. We have done our utmost in the world, failing or succeeding, and now we stand within the sanctuary, before the Eternal, and what we have done or not done is swallowed up in mystery. We have worked, laying our wills against the world; now we worship, that God may lay His

will against us. We have entered into the making of the
world, but that is not enough; we desire God to enter into
the making of our life.

—Sammuel H. Miller

SACRED ORGAN MUSIC

ENTERING INTO HIS COURTS WITH PRAISE
CALL TO WORSHIP

Leader: Christ brings us together in his love and unifies
us by his love to be his people.

People: Because he loves us, we seek to love him with
all our heart, soul, mind, and strength.

Leader: Christ inspires us through his love to be loving
people.

People: Because he loves us all, we love each other.

Leader: Thus we gather as a community of faith, the
church of Jesus Christ, the family of God.

People: We give thanks to God for reconciling us to himself, and to each other, and we take on ourselves Christ's claims of love and reconciliation.

INVOCATION
HYMN   "Crown Him with Many Crowns"   Elvey
GREETING THE WORSHIPERS
ANTHEM

HEARING HIS WORD
AN OLD TESTAMENT READING *(In unison)*   Psalm 37:3-6
A NEW TESTAMENT READING   Luke 17:22-37

RETURNING HIS GIFTS
HYMN   "To Worship, Work, and Witness"   Webb
THE MORNING OFFERING
Offertory Prayer
Organ Offertory

EXPRESSING OUR COMMITMENT TO HIM
PRESENTATION OF NEW DEACONS

COVENANT OF ORDINATION AND INSTALLATION

Minister: Do you trust that you are truly called by God to the ministry of a deacon in this church?

Deacons: I do so trust.

Minister: Are you committed to ministering to those in need, to explaining salvation in Jesus, and to calling forth greater discipleship to Christ?

Deacons: By God's grace, I am so committed.

Minister: Will you seek to provide an upright example by your total like—your words, your attitude, your behavior, and your family life—that will point others to Christ?

Deacons: I will, with God's help.

Minister: Are you committed to upholding the fellowship of Christ's church in *(name of church),* doing all you can to support, affirm, and undergird its ministry through your presence, your possessions, and your witness?

Deacons: I am, the Lord being my inspiration and my helper.

Minister: These are the people you have elected.
You have heard their declaration of their readiness to serve in the office of deacon.
I ask you, the church, to declare your affirmation. *(congregation stands.)*

Minister: We are not sufficient in and of ourselves. Our strength comes from God. Do you trust that these people are, by the grace of God, worthy to be installed and ordained as deacons?

People: *We trust they are worthy. To God be the glory!*

LAYING ON OF HANDS
ORDINATION PRAYER
AFFIRMATION OF DEACONS

Minister: I hereby declare that *(names)* are duly ordained as deacons, and that they, along with *(names)* are installed in this office of active deacons.

> May we as minister, deacons, and church strive
> together to seek God's will and labor to fulfill it.

ANTHEM
MESSAGE
HYMN   "O Jesus, I Have Promised"   Mann
PRESENTATION OF NEW MEMBERS
SPOKEN BENEDICATION
ORGAN DISMISSAL

Workers' Installation and Dedication Sunday

Another Sunday similar to the deacons' day is that of the general workers and teachers in a church. This order of worship is designed to illustrate the timing and content of a workers' installation/dedication.

The litany with the leaders is easy for a large group scattered throughout the sanctuary to enter into together. The people have an important response, for which they stand. The silent meditation provides quiet, personal time of reflection and dedication. The headings are from the second hymn.

Additional congregational participation includes the offertory response, using one stanza of a hymn, and the corporate benediction as the words of parting.

THE WORSHIP OF GOD
COME, ALL CHRISTIANS

CHORAL PRELUDE
WELCOME TO THE WORSHIPERS
SUMMONS TO WORSHIP

In the name of Jesus Christ I greet you.
In the loving of the Suffering Son of God I call your attention to the purpose of this hour.
In the presence of the abiding Holy Spirit I invite you to worship in Spirit and in truth.
In the intention of our resurrected Lord I challenge you to be open to God, to one another, and to yourself and the

direction of Christ for his church in this hour.

HYMN   "Rise Up, O Men of God"   Williams

INVOCATION

BE COMMITTED TO THE SERVICE OF THE LORD

THE OLD TESTAMENT READING   Deuteronomy 6:4-9
THE NEW TESTAMENT READING   Romans 6:12-14
RECOGNITION OF ALL CHURCH LEADERS
AFFIRMATION OF INSTALLATION AND DEDICATION

Minister: Eternal God, our Father, we realize that this work to which we dedicate ourselves is your work: that we have been called to it by you; that without you, we can do nothing; but that with you all things are possible. Therefore, trusting in your grace: to help growing persons know and love and serve you,

Leaders: We consecrate ourselves, our Father.

Minister: To help others to understand, appreciate, and accept Jesus Christ as Savior and Lord,

Leaders: We consecrate ourselves, our Father.

Minister: To help others grow into persons who have the breadth of sympathy which Jesus had, the radiance of his joy, the winsomeness of his love,

Leaders: We consecrate ourselves, our Father.

Minister: To encourage others to participate in the life and work, the mission and ministry of our church,

Leaders: We consecrate ourselves, our Father.

Minister: To share with growing persons our understanding and appreciation of the Bible as the living Word of God,

Leaders: We consecrate ourselves, our Father.

Minister: Now as you are formally installed into your respective places of leadership, it is expected that you will remember you are serving Christ and his church and that to whom much has been given, much is expected.

Leaders: Bless us, our Father, in the renewal of our dedi-
          cation to you. May we use the gifts which you
          have given us to undergird each other. May we
          daily share your love with all whom we serve in
          your name.

People: *We accept you as our educational leaders, and*
          we pledge our response to your guidance, so
          that we together may grow in grace, in knowl-
          edge, and in glorifying our God through Jesus
          Christ, our Lord.

SILENT MEDITATION

May we remember that the Lord sees and knows who we
are. He has made us to love him and serve him. He has
given us our calling to be his disciples. He asks us to make
as our profession that he is our Lord. He directs us to use
our careers as our means of supporting our calling and
profession and as our basic platform for our Christian witness. With this understanding of who we are, may we seek
to dedicate all phases of our lives to serve him, including
the leadership and fellowship shared in this Christian fellowship.

PRAYER OF DEDICATION

MAKE YOUR LIVES FOR HIM MORE FITTED
HYMN   "Come, All Christians, Be Committed"   Wood
MORNING OFFERING
    Offertory Prayer
    Handbell Offertory
    Offertory Response   "All Things Are Thine"
        (Hymn: "Jesus Shall Reign"; tune: DUKE STREET)
            "All things are Thine: no gift have we
            Lord of all gifts, to offer Thee;
            And hence with grateful hearts today,
            Thine own before Thy feet we lay."

TUNE YOUR HEARTS WITH ONE ACCORD
ANTHEM

TURN AWAY FROM SIN AND SADNESS
MESSAGE

BE TRANSFORMED WITH LIFE ANEW
A CALL TO DECISION AND DEDICATION
HYMN   "Take My Life, and Let It Be"   Anonymous
PRESENTATION OF NEW MEMBERS
WORDS OF PARTING

Leader: Go forth, knowing that you are daily loved by God and daily receiving the potential gift of being made right with God.

People: We go forth to exhibit a special quality of living—renewed by being set right with God, sustained by the love of God, redirected by this holy experience of worship, and recharged for a life of joyful, committed Christian service.

Leader: In a world where envy, criticism, violence, jealousy, hatred and mistrust reign supreme, we go forth to express the love and life that is unique to God.

People: We go forth to live God's love, hoping thereby to bring peace, joy, compassion, and love to our world, and to our lives.

Leader: Amen.

People: Amen.

ORGAN DISMISSAL

Reformation Sunday

Reformation Sunday, the last Sunday in October, is an important time of remembering what Martin Luther did more than four and a half centuries ago. Based on Luther's concern, this day is a time of focusing on repentance instead of penance. The headings and meditation time emphasize the confession/repentance needs.

The call to worship is adapted from Dr. John R. Claypool's work, and the benediction is adapted from the work of Fred M. Reese, Jr., in *Ventures in Worship, Vol. II,* edited by David James Randolph. Copyright © 1970 by Abingdon Press, p. 106. Used by permission.

THE WORSHIP OF GOD

THE PEOPLE OF GOD GATHER

SACRED ORGAN MUSIC

This hour of worship can become a flat, empty time when mind and emotions are put in neutral. Out of habit, sense of obligation, or pressure from family or peers, we may come to a holy place for wrong reasons. God has created us with the desire and potential for communion with him. This hour is designed to provide each of us the unique opportunity of worshiping God corporately. Rejoice in the presence of God! Remember that others have come here to worship. Realize an authentic, personal reason for being in this place. Use this hour to encounter God!

—Robert W. Bailey

TO LIFT UP PRAISE

CORPORATE CALL TO WORSHIP

Leader: God lives!

People: His Spirit dwells among us!

Leader: Life lives!

People: Salvation has come to us through Jesus Christ!

Leader: Hope lives!

People: A new day has dawned before us!

Leader: Forgiveness lives!

People: Our sins and mistakes cannot overcome us.

Leader: Love lives!

People: Death can never destroy us!

Leader: We live!

People: New and abundant life is possible through Jesus Christ!

Leader: Hallelujah!

People: Hallelujah!

Unison: Hallelujah!

HYMN "Joyful, Joyful, We Adore Thee" Beethoven

INVOCATION

WELCOME TO THE WORSHIPERS

TO READ THE WORD

THE WORD OF GOD FROM THE NEW TESTAMENT 1 John 1:5-10

TO CONFESS SINS

ANTHEM

SILENT MEDITATION

How our lives do ache! We are often overcome by our own sinfulness. We too often forget about God's presence, God's forgiveness, God's comfort, and God's assurance. As we remember and confess our sins, may we also become aware of all God offers us.

TO SEEK FORGIVENESS
THE MORNING PRAYER

TO GIVE TITHES AND OFFERINGS
HYMN   "Dear Lord and Father of Mankind"   Maker
THE MORNING OFFERING
Offertory Prayer
Piano Offertory

TO HEAR THE GOOD NEWS
ANTHEM
MESSAGE

TO MAKE A COMMITMENT
HYMN   "I Have Decided to Follow Jesus"   arr. by Reynolds
PRESENTATION OF NEW MEMBERS

THE PEOPLE OF GOD DEPART TO PROCLAIM REDEMPTION AND RELEASE TO THE WORLD
CORPORATE BENEDICTION

Leader: We are a forgiven people.
People: We are a called people.
Leader: We are a redeemed people.
People: We are a chosen people.
Leader: We are a covenant people.
People: We are a servant people.
Unison: We are a people of faith in the lordship of Jesus Christ.
Leader: In the confidence and presence of our Lord's abiding Spirit, go into his world to express your faith. Amen.

CHORAL RESPONSE
ORGAN DISMISSAL

Thanksgiving Sunday

This traditional American holiday can take an added meaning by planning another worship experience on the theme of gratitude either the Sunday before or the Sunday after Thanksgiving.

The section headings in the worship guide spin off the hymn, "Now Thank We All Our God." The opening sentences and responsive offertory prayer continue the theme and allow congregational participation in expressing thanksgiving. The musical response adds to the celebration that all we have comes from God. The parting word of gratitude enables the people to depart with the awareness that thanksgiving needs to be a daily diet for all believers.

At a time of the year when stewardship emphasis is typical, this sermon can be an asset to greater dependence upon God and greater stewardship through greater gratitude.

THE WORSHIP OF GOD

SACRED ORGAN MUSIC
THE CHIMING OF THE HOUR

NOW THANK WE ALL OUR GOD
OPENING SENTENCES

Leader: All people, make a joyful noise unto the Lord!

People: Serve him with thankfulness and come before him, singing with joy!

Leader: Try to realize what this means—the Lord is God!

People: It is he that made us. All that is was made by him!

Leader: Enter into his gates with thanksgiving and into his courts with praise.
Be grateful to him and bless his name.

People: And now we thank thee, our God, and praise your glorious name.

INVOCATION

HYMN   "Come, Ye Thankful People, Come"   Elvey

NOW WE LIFT OURSELVES TO HIM

A TIME FOR GREETING

AN OLD TESTAMENT READING   Exodus 16:1-8

A NEW TESTAMENT READING   Luke 21:1-4

DUET

PRAYER OF THANKSGIVING

NOW WE RETURN OUR GIFTS OF LOVE

HYMN   "We Gather Together"   Kremser

THE MORNING OFFERING

Offertory Prayer

Leader: We thank you for all your many good gifts, O God,

˙People: Help us to use them wisely.

Leader: We dedicate your tithes and our offerings in Christ's church, O God,

People: Help them to be used to glorify your name.

Leader: We consecrate our lives to be fit for your service,

People: Help us to withhold nothing from you.

Leader: We give you our best, our all, with joyful thanksgiving,

People: Help us not to begrudge our gift nor to belittle one who gives less than we give.

Unison: Help us to be good stewards of all you have
entrusted to us. Amen.
Organ Offertory
Congregational Response
"Bless Thou the gifts our hands have brought;
    Bless Thou the work our hearts have planned;
Ours is the faith, the will, the thought;
    The rest, O God, is in Thy hand. Amen."

NOW WE EXPRESS OUR COMMITMENT TO HIM

ANTHEM
MESSAGE
HYMN   "I Gave My Life for Thee"   Bliss
THE PRESENTATION OF NEW MEMBERS
A PARTING WORD OF GRATITUDE
Leader: Blessed are you, O Lord, the God of Israel our
Father, for ever and ever.
People: And now we thank you, our God, and praise your
glorious name by the way in which we live in
your world.
CHORAL AMEN
ORGAN DISMISSAL

Baptism and the Lord's Supper

Baptism and the Lord's Supper are the two ordinances of Baptists. They should be celebrated together as much as possible. There may be times of having the Lord's Supper alone, but Baptism should always be followed by the Lord's Supper. The hour of worship should be so carefully planned that the two events together do not exceed the hour. If the Lord's Supper is celebrated alone, it should not be tacked on the end of regular worship but should be the sole, central theme of worship.

The worship guide suggests that the worship leader begin the worship event so that the minister and baptismal candidates can be dressed for the baptism. From the water, the minister leads in worship from the "Declaration of Baptism" through the "Baptismal Prayer." While these portions of the worship are brief, they are invaluable teaching moments and must be carefully planned and thought out.

The congregation joins in the opening sentences and the "Litany of Dedication" which preceeds the celebration of the Lord's Supper. The parting hymn is varied among six or eight hymns, including, "Blest Be the Tie." The other three hymns tie in with the theme of baptism and the Lord's Supper, just as the hymns each Sunday tie in with the specific theme of that week.

THE WORSHIP OF GOD

THE CELEBRATION OF BAPTISM AND THE LORD'S SUPPER
SACRED INSTRUMENTAL MUSIC

PRAISING THE AUTHOR OF THE CELEBRATION
OPENING SENTENCES

Leader: We believe God sends us into his world to exercise compassion. In his concern for the well-being of the universe, God has never forgotten the needs of individuals.

People: Christ gives strength and endurance to every person, based on the witness of their lives, by the ministry of their lives in his name.

Leader: We believe God calls the church of Christ to be people who here and now show personal concern for other persons. We believe God sends us into his world to risk our own comfort and peace as we express compassion for our neighbors.

People: To give to them, and receive from them, accepting everyone we meet as a person; to be sensitive to those who suffer in body or mind; and to help and accept help in ways that affirm dignity.

Leader: We believe God has a purpose for each Christian and a purpose for Christ's church collectively, a purpose that lends joy and consistency to our living. In inspiration and hope we encounter him in this hour so that we might realize more fully and respond more completely to our purpose.

INVOCATION
HYMN   "O Church of God, Triumphant"   Smart
GREETING THE WORSHIPERS

PARTICIPATION IN CHRIST'S WITNESS
THE DECLARATION OF BAPTISM
THE CANDIDATES
  (names listed here)

REFLECTING ON THE CELEBRATION
RESPONSIVE READING

CHARGE TO THE CHURCH
BAPTISMAL PRAYER
ANTHEM

BRINGING OUR GIFTS FOR THE CELEBRATION
HYMN   "Where Can We Find Thee, Lord, So Near"
(Hymn: "When I Survey the Wondrous Cross"; tune: HAMBURG)
MORNING OFFERING
   Offertory Prayer
   Instrumental Offertory
ANTHEM
READING OF THE WORD   3 John 1-14
MEDITATION
HYMN   "Beneath the Cross of Jesus"   Maker
PRESENTATION OF NEW MEMBERS

PARTICIPATING IN THE CELEBRATION
LITANY OF DEDICATION

Leader: Thou shall love the Lord thy God:
People: I will love the Lord my God with all my heart.
Leader: Thou shall love the Lord thy God:
People: I will love the Lord my God with all my soul.
Leader: Thou shall love the Lord thy God:
People: I will love the Lord my God with all my strength.
Leader: Thou shall love the Lord thy God:
People: I will love the Lord my God with all my mind.
Leader: Thou shall love thy neighbor as thyself:
People: I will love my neighbor as myself, even as Christ
          loves me and gave himself for me.

PARTAKING FROM THE TABLE
   Receiving the Bread
   Receiving the Cup

CELEBRATING THE NEW LIFE AMONG US
THE ACKNOWLEDGEMENT OF NEW MEMBERS
A PARTING HYMN

   "God be with you till we meet again!

By his counsels guide, uphold you,
With his sheep securely fold you;
God be with you till we meet again!
God be with you till we meet again!
'Neath his wings protecting hide you,
Daily manna still provide you;
God be with you till we meet again!"

Missions Sunday

Nearly every church observes one or more missions Sundays during the course of a year. This order of worship draws together the several components of such a worship experience.

In four unique ways the congregation is led to express itself on missions through the "Opening Sentences," through "A Call to Prayer Missions," through the "Offertory Sentences," and through the "Corporate Benediction."

In addition to the hymns on missions, a lay leader speaks briefly to reflect on the importance of missions. Frequently it helps to hear the same truth the minister proclaims from the words of a respected lay person. Of course this assignment must be brief, and the lay person must realize the time limitations in advance.

Once again the headings spell out the theme and draw together the various aspects of worship.

THE WORSHIP OF GOD

SACRED ORGAN MUSIC

THE SOURCE OF ABUNDANT LIFE
OPENING SENTENCES

Leader: We come seeking meaning for our lives, wondering where we can find a loom on which to weave the patterns of our tomorrow.

People: All of us seek truth for our lives.

Leader: We come with questions and uncertainty, searching for the anvil on which we can shape tools for tomorrow's harvest.

People: All of us seek power for living.

Leader: We come with a multitude of needs without and within—our families need us, our church needs us, our community needs us, our nation needs us, a lost world needs us—and *we* need, questioning where we can find power into which we can plug our lives.

People: All of us seek purpose in living.

Leader: We come with a vital heritage, encircled by a great cloud of witnesses, looking for guideposts at the crossroads that will direct us to new avenues of service.

Unison: We seek meaning in God's love,
              truth in his Word,
              power in his Spirit, and
              purpose in his commission which
                  sends us to the uttermost parts of
                  the earth.

HYMN   "Ye Christian Heralds"   Hatton
INVOCATION
GREETING THE WORSHIPERS
ANTHEM

THE AUTHOR OF OUR WITNESS

OLD TESTAMENT READING   Deuteronomy 30:11-14
NEW TESTAMENT READING   Romans 10:5-15
REFLECTION ON MISSIONS
A CALL TO PRAYER ON MISSIONS

Leader: We believe under Christ that we have a commission to be on mission in his Name.

People: The world is changing so quickly, can we still feel the enthusiasm we once did for missions?

Leader: We believe that Christ calls us to responsible praying for mission support.
People: Pessimism looms heavy around the world—do we really make any difference?
Leader: We believe we are charged to give sacrificially for mission support.
People: Inflation takes its toll on us and governments help in so many ways—is it still necessary for us to give?
Leader: We believe we are directed to become involved personally in sharing the name of Christ.
People: Our schedules are already so filled with important things—can we spend any time or energy sharing Christ?
Leader: We are needed today more than ever before for the cause of Christ.
Unison: May Christ open our minds so we may perceive authentic needs
          May he open our eyes that we may see clearly the suffering
          May he open our hearts that we may respond with compassion
          May he open our hands that we may use our strength and resources.
          May Christ help us be faithful stewards on mission in his name!

PRAYER ON MISSIONS

THE GIVER OF GOOD GIFTS

HYMN   "Jesus, Friend of Thronging Pilgrims"
              (Hymn: "Angels, From the Realms of Glory";
                        tune: REGENT SQUARE)

MORNING OFFERING
   Offertory Sentences

Leader: We celebrate what the Father has entrusted to us,
People: Help us to be worthy stewards, O God.

Leader: We acknowledge that all we have comes from
          the Father,
People: Help us to be worthy stewards, O God.
Leader: We realize that we own nothing, but merely use
          the Father's gifts for a time,
People: Help us to be worthy stewards, O God.
Leader: We know that the world awaits the gifts of our
          lives, energy, and material means so that they
          might discover the redeeming power of Jesus
          Christ,
People: Help us to be worthy stewards, O God.

Organ Offertory

THE TEACHER OF GENUINE DISCIPLESHIP

ANTHEM
MESSAGE
HYMN   "Dear Lord and Father of Mankind"   Maker
PRESENTATION OF NEW MEMBERS
BENEDICTION
ORGAN DISMISSAL

Conclusion

The idea of new ways in Christian worship is actually not new at all to the Christian faith. From the outset of man's coming to know God in Jesus Christ, the intent was to encounter God in a life-changing manner in worship. The reality is that the celebration of modern religion has often become more people-centered than God-centered. More emphasis has been placed on programs, budgets, organizations, and buildings than on meditation, encounter, repentance, and God-led worship and lives.

Worship is not a gimmick for coercing something from the worshipers. Innovative worship forms are not a means of pumping new spirit into a decaying institution. Authentic worship is an occasion of enabling people from all walks of life to enter into an obvious presence of God in the company of believers so that God's Word and intent might be made clear.

Altering the order of worship weekly will be to no avail unless the worship is theologically and biblically sound. On the other hand, the goal of authentic worship may not be achieved unless some variety and freshness are incorporated into the worship experience on a regular basis.

This book is not intended to be complete in any sense. Rather, the hope is that it will stir creativity both among those who plan worship and all those who worship. Worship is exciting and life-transforming. When you prepare your heart and order the worship event in your church in accord with the Holy Spirit's leading, you can overcome the distractions of corporate worship and help provide stimulating encounter with the living God!

Bibliography

Baillie, John, *A Diary of Private Prayer.* New York: Charles Scribner's Sons, 1949.

Barry, James C. and Jack Gulledge, eds., *Ideas for Effective Worship Services.* Nashville: Convention Press, 1977.

Christensen, James L., *Contemporary Worship Services.* Old Tappan, N.J.: Fleming H. Revell Company, 1970.

Christensen, James L., *New Ways to Worship.* Old Tappan, N.J.: Fleming H. Revell Company, 1973.

Davies, Horton, *Christian Worship.* New York: Abingdon Press, 1957.

Hoon, Paul W., *The Integrity of Worship.* New York: Abingdon Press, 1971.

Keir, Thomas H., *The Word in Worship.* New York: Oxford University Press, 1962.

Killinger, John, *Leave It to the Spirit.* New York: Harper and Row, 1971.

Quoist, Michel, *Prayers.* New York: Sheed and Ward, 1963.

Randolph, David James, *Ventures in Worship, Vols. I,II,III,* Nashville: Abingdon Press, 1969, 1970, 1973.

Snyder, Ross, *Contemporary Celebration.* Nashville: Abingdon Press, 1971.

Segler, Franklin M., *Christian Worship.* Nashville: Broadman Press, 1967.

Sparkman, G. Temp, *Writing Your Own Worship Materials.* Valley Forge: Judson Press, 1980.

Thielicke, Helmut, *The Trouble with the Church.* New York: Harper and Row, 1965.

Underhill, Evelyn, *Worship.* New York: Harper and Row, 1957.

Walker, Daniel D., *Enemy in the Pew?* New York: Harper and Row, 1967.

Willimon, William H., *Worship as Pastoral Care.* New York: Abingdon Press, 1979.

Winward, Stephen F., *The Reformation of Our Worship.* Richmond, Va.: John Knox Press, 1965.